PARADISE
LOST

Mollie Bach

ARPress
ILLUMINATING IDEAS
EMPOWERING VOICES

ARPress
45 Dan Road Suite 5
Canton MA 02021

Hotline: 1(888) 821-0229
Fax: 1(508) 545-7580

Ordering Information:
Quantity sales. Special discounts are available on quantity purchases by corporations, associations, and others. For details, contact the publisher at the address above.

Printed in the United States of America.

ISBN-13:	Softcover	979-8-89389-148-5
	eBook	979-8-89389-164-5

Library of Congress Control Number: 2024914263

Prologue

November 1980

Daddy didn't come. The fat lady came instead. It was raining. I watched
as her hair stuck to her face. She looked so silly.

'Your father's not coming to meet you today. Come home with me,' she said.

'I'm not coming home with you.'

'Your mother's waiting for you.'

I was cold.

'My mother is never waiting for me.'

I looked at the fat lady. She was very good at cleaning. She did it so
often. A dewdrop fell from her nose. It was gooey.

She was holding my hand tightly.

I ran up the stairs of our house in Pembridge Square. Frumps, my
black Labrador, leapt on me. She smelt of bones.

Mummy was in bed. It was her favourite place.

The fire in the lounge lit up the room.

I heard my mother calling me. I walked upstairs – across the wooden
floor. I went into her bedroom. She smelt of gin.

I was going to school in the country, she told me. 'It'll be a nice
school where you can ride horses. You'd like that, wouldn't you?'

'I like it here.'

'No, no! London smells. You'll have lots of friends. There will be green fields.'

'I have friends here.'

'Not nice friends you haven't.'

Drink fell into a glass. It went into her throat. I lay on the bed. Mummy left the room. I smelt Frumps. I put my arm around her neck. I buried my head between her ears. I lay with her. We'd hide under the stairs. Mummy wouldn't miss us. She'd go into the glass. She always did.

I heard her dropping things. She would sleep soon. We crept downstairs. I saw her lying on the floor. Her mouth was open.

I put Frumps' basket and bones into the back of the cupboard. I took chocolate cake in and shut the door. I lay in the black cupboard. I could hear the sounds.

At last she shouted, 'Where are you? Where are you, Judith?'

I heard the sound of shattering glass. My mother stumbled and fell. I was glad.

I hoped the glass would cut her all up. She wouldn't be there.

'Where are you?' I heard her shout.

In the corner, there was an enormous spider's web. I gazed at it. I saw a captured fly. A head emerged between its wings. It was a hideous creature half-human, half-fly. It was so dark I opened the door. I saw my mother with a knife, coming out of the kitchen.

'I want to stay here with you! Please let me stay with you!' I screamed. Frumps ran out of the cupboard towards my mother then Frumps was hurt and bleeding. I didn't know how to help her.

I was sent to school. I watched the hot wheels – rat-a-tat-tat they went; round and round they whirled. The carriage was full of girls wearing the same clothes that I had on. The teacher, Miss Humphries, was strict and told me to close the window. It took ages and ages to get to Dorset.

When I saw the school, I thought it must be the oldest house in the whole world. We drove down the drive. There were horses on either side and lots of daisies. The grass was green. We went through a big door.

An old, fat lady, called Mrs Canning came and sat next to us. I missed Frumps. I cried; everyone stared. I was taken to a bedroom, called a dormitory. It had twelve beds in it. I was the only one who was seven; everyone else was eight. I missed Frumps. I wanted some sweets, but there weren't any. My trunk was on my bed. A lady helped me unpack. She said the trunk would go away until the end of term. I felt hot when she said that. The end of term – I wouldn't see Frumps or Daddy until the end of term. I cried.

Boils came up on my body. There were lots of them. Green stuff came out of them. Matron lanced them. It hurt a lot. I climbed trees.

One day, I went home. Frumps was gone.

CHAPTER ONE

14 April 2000

Notting Hill Gate was quiet that morning as Judith waited for the bus. When it arrived, she boarded and went upstairs to find a seat by the window so she could think about the exhibition. There was a fluttering of excitement in her stomach; that's what van Gogh could do to her. H.

She leapt off the bus into bright sunshine. The doors of the Royal Academy stood in front of her, evoking vivid memories of her time as a student. She'd gone there straight from school, when she was just seventeen. The signs to the exhibition were clearly marked, and she followed them without hesitation.

Someone was looking down at her. That's what people did; they looked. She was used to it. Only this time she felt compelled to return the gaze. That was unusual. His brown curly hair defined his facial features, angular and ragged. They cut through her, leaving her feeling bare, bereft. He moved on to the next painting, and once there, he looked again. There was a gladness in his gaze.

Where, she wondered, did this gladness come from? What was its source? And why so suddenly? He was there; it was what she wanted. Supposing he didn't speak? This was a gallery, after all – but he had to, didn't he? He couldn't just slide into her and silently walk away.

She looked round. He was behind her now, with his huge hands and long thick fingers. She asked him why he was there.

My doctorate,' he replied.

'Van Gogh is your subject?'

'Yes, his insanity; that's my subject.'

The gallery filled up with people. He drifted away; yet, whenever she looked round, he was there.

Why aren't you inside me now? Why don't you know? she thought as her eyes went from the paintings to his face and back again. He wrote notes. She drew. They were close enough to feel each other's breath. That was how they got through the exhibition together – and yet apart. This focus made it bearable until they got out into sunshine. Then things began to drift, to get hazy. It was the longing, the lingering, the waiting, and the fear that it might not happen.

How would it be if it didn't happen? she wondered.

There were people everywhere. She ran to the Tube because it was underground. He followed and grabbed her arm. There was no resistance, only connection. His mobile phone rang.

'Annabel. No. Lunch is impossible.'

He held her wrist. It was sore. Seeing, at once, the line and the cut, he took it to his mouth and kissed the scar. He pushed her sleeve up. She tried to pull her arm away in embarrassment, but he held it more tightly. The underground was full of people.

Judith's secret was out. The whole of London could see. It was no secret any more. Everyone knew. The whole world knew. He gazed at the patterns on her skin; she made patterns sometimes. He touched them with his fingers. There was a softness, and then the longing and the wanting began. He took her face in his huge hands and held it, exploring the skin, the eyes, the mouth. She trembled. She wanted him then and there, in that place. He pulled her up the stairs. There was a taxi close by. He hailed it. They got in.

'Lancaster Road, off Ladbroke Grove, just off Portobello Road!' he shouted at the man, before slamming the door.

She pushed against him. He was hard.

'No. Not here, not now,' he murmured.

The taxi stopped. He threw some money at the driver and ran up the steps of the house. Judith tripped over everything in the hall. She saw packed suitcases, easels, and a pile of line drawings. But he dragged her through the chaos of it all into a kitchen filled with copper saucepans. Jars and glasses crashed to the floor as he made a space for her on the table. It seemed he'd turned to some base metal that moved and melted around and within her. There was simply an intense presence that removed everything in its path; everything that prevented penetration had to be smashed and destroyed. She'd been swept away, taken somewhere entirely different – to a holy, sacred place away.

It was over. Suddenly, his mobile phone went again.

'You know I'm going away, Annabel. I told you.'

Judith left the table and wandered around the house, which was painted white from top to bottom. The door of the studio stood ajar. There she found huge canvases depicting human forms. The paint seemed to have been scraped on in lumps and then dabbed on. Tubes of colour – scarlet, indigo, black, and putty – lay open, exposed to the elements. The smell of linseed permeated the air, the scent of turpentine. These were the smells she'd grown up with.

He placed a mug of scalding tea in her hand. 'I've a holiday arranged. I can't cancel it's part of my study I'm going to stay in a gite near Arles… You can't arrive in my life and make me cancel.'

'You go,' she murmured, knowing it to be impossible.

He took hold of her arm. They reached the bedroom. He stroked her shoulder, her arms, her mouth. She opened, and he entered, sliding around her being and into it. The waves and movement of the sea, the tides and the saltiness of desire moved between them. His sweat burnt the cuts that were sore from his rubbing. The stubble on his chin made her cry out at times when he forgot that they weren't forged together by molten metal but that they were separate beings and that their hearts existed in separate chambers. It was over.

There were practical questions – her jeep, his jeep, or both jeeps? They could take twice as many canvases and more paint. She knew that she would go with him wherever he wanted.

Her father indulged her, with the loan of the jeep. He asked very few questions; he was always pleased when she escaped with her paints and her easels.

Claude gave her everything she required to arrive safely at the villa. He set the Tom-Tom for her so there was no doubt that she would find her way. It was the kind of freedom she'd never imagined. She felt brave and bereft at the same time. It was hot. The sun beat down on the back of her neck for the whole journey. She covered her head completely with a soft muslin shawl.

The Tom-Tom told her that she had another fifty kilometres to go before reaching the gîte. Storm clouds gathered as the sky turned crimson with streaks of vermilion and magenta; it ignited memories of both blood and bathroom.

When she arrived at the gîte, Claude emerged to greet her. His movements flowed seamlessly, without effort.

She wanted this, crazy and impulsive though it was. Claude took her into the large garden, where he grasped hold of her face with his huge hands and looked into her eyes. It was as if he could see into her brain and beyond, into the caverns of her mind.

The house itself was simple. Whitewash covered the walls. The kitchen contained a large oak table. There some French cupboards painted green with tiny flowers on the doors and a huge range to cook on.

A room with French windows that opened out onto the garden dominated downstairs. Two sofas, covered with heavy linen in shades of stone and dark blue, filled the living area. This was the place she wanted to be – forever here with him. He nuzzled into her neck and then walked away only to return moments later. It was as if he couldn't go until afterwards; only then could he go away and leave her alone until the next time.

There was a studio at the end of the house where they set up their paints and all the rest of the paraphernalia that goes with being an artist – easels, turpentine, brushes, and so on. He stroked her hair as she painted. She surrendered, relieved that bedtime had arrived.

When she woke, it was 9 a.m. She looked up from her bed, surveyed the room, and found herself alone. The window was small and opened onto a view of fields with clusters of wild flowers.

A voice downstairs shouted, 'Bonjour!'

She pulled on a pair of trousers and ran to find a plump grey-haired lady making coffee. Warm croissants sat on the table beside a lump of French butter and a pot of apricot preserve.

'Bonjour. Parlez-vous Anglais?' enquired Claude.

'Oui, oui, Monsieur,' replied the grey-haired lady. 'Un peu, un peu.' They sat down to bowls of café au lait and croissants.

'I come with the house, Monsieur. I cook, I clean for the next fourteen days,' she said. Her heavy French accent made Judith smile.

'Thank you, merci, merci, madame,' she replied, feeling safer somehow, reassured that all would be taken care of by this large lovely soul whose name was Marie.

After breakfast, the two of them went out for a long walk in the French countryside, near Arles. The intensity of colour seeped through Judith's skin, the aroma of fresh lavender that grew in the fields where they wandered intoxicated her.

She observed the way the light fell on the fields where van Gogh had painted. This was the place that inspired his greatest work. Claude told her that the artist had been the subject of his thesis, and that he'd become increasingly fascinated by the various facets of van Gogh's personality – especially his epilepsy and the insanity that led to his suicide. Walking with this stranger in this strange land felt like the most natural thing in the world to her.

She wondered once more if this was how it had all begun. Was there a how to these things? Was there a moment there in that field when Claude fell into danger? 'Provence,' he said – as if reading her thoughts – 'has its dangers, not just for van Gogh but for all of us. Every sense is heightened here.' Despite this, her natural anxiety softened like wax in the midday sun.

'We'd better be getting back,' Claude murmured, stroking her hands, her eyes, her face.

At that very moment, Claude's mobile rang, and he picked it up.

'John, John, that's you, isn't it? … Well. I'm here in Provence, near Arles, as you asked me to be. My wine-tasting course is over.'

'No, there's a girl here who came yesterday. Her name's Judith.' She couldn't help but smile. She often smiled in the wrong places and the wrong time. It was hot. It all felt unreal, and in a way, it was. There she was in this French house with this strange man.

Marie produced food and wine, but no one knew what to say or how to respond. They ate silently.

Suddenly, Judith's mobile phone rang, and she picked it up.

'Hello, it's me. Are you okay?' Judith knew her father's voice at once. 'Shall I come home?'

Claude grabbed the phone from her hand. 'No, no! Don't do that, for God's sake. Stay here. You have no idea,' he said.

She felt sad for him, so sad. 'Well, if you're sure.'

'Yes, I'm bloody sure.'

She knew that she would stay, even without the knives. She'd left them wrapped up in her bedroom drawer in London. They'd be there when she returned.

Claude's phone rang. There was a woman's voice and the sound of sobbing. 'No, Annabel. I'm not coming back – not now. Yes, go to the job in Hanford. Take it.'

Judith went away into the garden and sat by the stream watching the water rise and fall. He came out eventually and told her that Annabel had held him in some safe place, but it was not what he needed now. She realized that this man felt smothered. She gasped and felt her throat restrict when he said that, if his mother had told him to throw himself headlong down a flight of stairs, he would have carried out her order at once, without either argument or hesitation. She sensed that Claude thought himself to be trash – nervous, weak-willed trash. It was this aspect of his personality that fascinated her because she identified with it immediately.

What sort of a human being am I? How will I ever know? she thought.

She went inside to paint and filled a vast canvas with a grey whitewash. This activity cleared her thoughts; it had always been that way, and she presumed that it always would be. She looked up and found him staring at her. It didn't disturb her because she was used to it. It was what men did.

'Do you teach van Gogh?'

'Not always, but he's my speciality. I wrote my dissertation on a specific aspect of his personality – the possible causes of his insanity and his inability to cope with rejection,' he replied.

This was just what she wanted to discover; this was the mystery she wanted to solve. This man might give her the key.

'What is it about him that draws you?' she asked.

'The way he opens minds.'

She responded by picking up her paintbrush and painting alone until it grew dark. Once in bed, she fell into a sleep that was filled with horrors – grey geese that couldn't stop flying until, eventually, their wings fell off. When she woke, she found Claude inside her. She wound herself round him and held him close as he moaned before the inevitable explosion that left her breathless, gasping for air.

There was a commotion downstairs, so they got dressed hurriedly and discovered an old man had arrived. Judith wondered who this man could be. Claude threw his arms around the man with the warmth that only a long association can bring.

'John, it's so good of you to come.'

'Claude, my boy, I wouldn't have missed this for the world. I promised I'd come, didn't I? So why on earth wouldn't I?' he replied.

This new man created a soft, congenial atmosphere, and fears evaporated in his presence. The dark mood that had hovered around both of them disappeared as though it had never existed.

Why, Judith wondered, *is it safe here without my knives?* She was unused to feeling safe. Perhaps she'd never felt safe before.

Marie prepared the meal. She too, was calmer since John's arrival.

He asked Judith where she lived, and she said London, Notting Hill Gate.

'Well, I live near there. Moscow Road in fact. Do you know it?' he asked.

'Oh yes, of course I do. The Greek Orthodox Church is nearby. It's magnificent.'

Claude lives in that area and, of course, Annabel.'

'I didn't know,' she replied, feeling inexplicably sad.

'Have you painted much?' John asked before handing her a cup of coffee.

'All my life or, at least, for as much of it as I can remember. I went to the Royal Academy when I left school. Painting is my life. It's the only thing that makes sense to me.'

'Go on,' he said.

He seemed so interested. She couldn't understand why. Why would anyone be interested in her? she wondered, watching intently as John lit his pipe. She thought him to be in his sixties, for his hair and beard were grey. Yet his blue eyes sparkled as she spoke. His skin reminded her of parchment; it was thin and rather crinkly.

'It's the sea in which I swim.'

'I'm a bit of a novice,' he confessed.

'What do you do?'

'I'm a student of human nature and of Carl Jung. I'm retired now, and so I read, eat, sleep, write, and go on wine-tasting courses whenever possible,' he replied, smiling from one side of his face to another.

'Jung, you say. Wasn't he something to do with Freud and psychoanalysis?'

That's right.'

'What did you study?' John enquired.

'Painting and sculpture at the Royal Academy. I was there for nearly four years after I left school, and then I did a couple of specialized courses concentrating on portraits. I only left last autumn.'

'Really? You must be very talented to have been accepted straight from school.'

'I don't know about that,' she said, smiling directly at him.

'We eat,' Marie commanded suddenly.

'Oui, oui, merci,' Claude replied. This kind of dual language had become normal banter between the two of them.

'I've known John all my life. He was a great friend of my father's,' Claude confided.

'He's lovely.' Claude smiled as she spoke, nodding in agreement. 'He exudes warmth, kindness even.'

'Yes, I suppose he does."

Claude's dark brown hair fell in wisps across his face. There was, she thought, a wildness about him. Memories of biting wind filled her mind.

'What are you …?'

'I'm thinking of cold wind.'

'Go on,' urged Claude.

'Images – they're just images that dance across my mind.'

'Is that what you paint?' he asked.

'It's what I draw,' she replied.

Judith had always loved drawing. She drew anything and everywhere.

She could often be seen sketching strangers on trains, and when she'd been at school, she'd drawn her teachers and her friends. In the process of drawing, she would come to know them better. She'd discovered the intimacy involved in artistic creation when she was still a child; it may have been the discovery that unleashed her genius.

'Do you make a living from art?' John enquired.

'I do and I don't.'

'What do you mean?'

'It engages me, it fascinates me…and sometimes I sell something,' she murmured.

Marie carried hot bowls of soup and bread down into the garden, and they gathered around the table.

'Van Gogh and Gauguin – tell us what you think about the relationship. It has always courted so much controversy in the art world,' John said as he began to eat.

'The level of creative energy would inevitably have caused an explosion,' replied Claude. 'They shared prostitutes. This created a powerful bond between them. It was the most influential relationship of van Gogh's life – apart from his mother. That's my opinion anyway.'

'Why do you say that about his mother?' asked John. 'Van Gogh's mother lost a child before he was born.'

Judith dropped the spoon onto the floor. The hot soup scalded her, but she didn't complain. She merely entered her internal world and withdrew all her emotional antennae from her environment and those who inhabited it. Silence fell around her like a veil.

'I never knew. Do you think that had an influence on him?'

'Undoubtedly,' Claude replied.

'Go on.'

'There is a school of thought, within the art world and beyond, that believes it was the cause of both his insanity and his epilepsy.'

'Please, go on.'

'When he was very, very young, van Gogh experienced deep hurt due to his mother's grief over the death of her firstborn child – he was a "replacement child", a term used by psychologists.'

Quicksilver entered Judith's head. She understood for the first time why she was inexorably drawn to this painter and why, when she was studying at the academy, she had frequently dreamt that they were married. It was an ongoing fantasy of hers; sometimes it was as if he held her paintbrush.

'Yes, replacement child is a term I'm very familiar with,' John replied.

'Van Gogh constantly craved to be loved,' Claude said with deep conviction.

Judith slowly stirred her soup, but she didn't eat it. She dipped a piece of bread into the hot liquid and watched closely as it sank from sight.

I wish I could sink like that, she thought.

'Very early in his life, he suffered from a feeling of abandonment that few, if any of us, could imagine,' Claude went on.

John took a chunk of French bread and tore it apart. Judith imagined there to be something violent about this action, so she poured herself a large glass of red wine, watching as the light played on the liquid.

'Many psychologists believe that this caused his extreme sensitivity to emotional rejection, which exacerbated the personality disorder that would eventually drive him to despair and suicide.'

'Rejection sensitivity caused him to cut his ear off. Is that what you're suggesting?' John replied while buttering his bread.

'It's the subject of my thesis – the degree to which Gauguin's rejection contributed to van Gogh's psychological disintegration.'

It was as if some invisible sword was cutting through Judith's mind, exposing areas that had previously been hidden. Eventually, after much soul-searching, John said he'd always found his paintings disturbing without understanding the reason. Van Gogh could, he said, make irises appear unhappy, sunflowers disturbed, and even the humble potato became melancholic under his influence.

Claude glanced across at Judith. She tried hard to smile but failed. She had lost her equilibrium; that had clearly been lost.

'It's lovely here,' he said.

'There is an intensity,' Judith murmured, realizing how easy it was to fall into van Gogh's web.

'Yes, indeed,' John replied.

'I want to learn more about the man. The paintings are the man, aren't they? she asked.

'To an extent, yes. I've looked at his paintings for as long as I can remember. I want to go deeper – to another level, if you like – and to discover more,' Claude said

'I'm interested in his insanity. He's a fascinating character study for me,' John replied.

'He mutilated himself whenever he was abandoned. They think it related to his relationship with his mother,' Claude went on, looking directly into Judith's eyes.

'I paint olive trees,' she said rapidly. Her words seemed to fall over one another she spoke so quickly.

'Always?' Claude asked in surprise.

'Yes.'

'Do you know why?' he asked.

'No. I put them in graveyards. I have some here.'

'You have? May I see them? I'd really love to.'

They wandered next door to the studio. There were three canvases in all. Two seemed almost complete, one hardly begun. The first one held a gnarled and broken tree in the centre of an immense graveyard.

'The branches appear to be falling!' John exclaimed, gazing closely at the canvas in front of him. 'The way you have individualized each gravestone is extraordinary. No two are the same, and yet there is the green on each – moss, ivy, or mould – there are so many shades of green. The way the ivy climbs the trunk of the tree…it's suffocating it and depriving it of nourishment. Is it for sale?'

'I've never thought of selling it,' she replied.

She looked at Claude and saw in her mind's eye his bony skull beneath the skin as a mass of tiny volcanoes filled with hot lava feeding nerve cells, divided and yet connected by a hot molten river.

Claude picked up another canvas. This time the olive trees were heavily detailed; sporadic gnarled trunks evolved into branches that tangled and wove round shades of red, brown, and green.

'Where do you find the force for the colour?' he asked.

'Within the tree itself,' she replied. 'The colours emerge from the tree, and then they become the tree.'

'There is no separation,' he replied, looking first at her and then at the painting.

'It's not clear,' she said slowly.

'It's very, very clear. Colour and form merge together, similar to the symbiosis you reveal so clearly in your painting,' Claude said as he picked up the third painting, which he propped up against the wall. He saw a bombed city. Among the ruins stood five massive olive trees.

'This picture isn't balanced; it's out of proportion,' he suddenly declared.

Judith moved to protect the painting from his gaze. 'War is out of proportion, isn't it? Is that not what makes it hideous?' she replied.

'It's absolute. It's extreme,'

'Yes, it's extreme. It obliterates everything – people, landscapes, and lives. It's out of proportion.'

'Why do birds suddenly appear?' asked Claude, looking into one of the cracks in the wall of the ruin.

'Because that's what they do. They appear as if from nowhere thoughts, ideas, and feelings emerge from nowhere. we can't see where they lead.'

'Wherever they lead, you must follow,' she insisted.

'That, and that alone, is truth,' Claude replied.

The next morning, John was alone in the kitchen, sipping hot coffee and eating bread smothered with apricot jam.

Judith saw him look up as if startled by something. She couldn't understand what.

'Have you known Claude long?' she asked eventually, after a very long uncomfortable silence.

'I was a friend of his parents. I'm a friend of Annabel's.'

At that moment, Claude emerged looking dishevelled, as if he'd not recovered from Judith and from the night that had passed.

'Are you okay?' she asked anxiously.

'I'm drunk on you.'

He left the room as if to remove himself from danger. John followed him, leaving Judith alone. She felt his absence immediately and wanted to follow, but she resisted the need. She sensed his distance. She knew that what she felt was fear. She wanted to go back to him so that she could experience his presence, his overwhelming need of her.

John came back to talk to her.

'There was an awful accident several years ago,' John explained gently. 'What happened?'

'They never recovered.'

'Who, who never recovered?'

'Claude's family.'

'Go on. I'm listening.'

'It's a long story. A car accident killed his parents and his sister. The driver was drunk. He got a few years.'

'Oh, my God, what about Claude's father?'

'He used to come and see me a lot at that time, but he had a job. So he had to carry on.'

'I see.'

'I probably shouldn't be telling you all this, but it's not confidential or anything. They were never clients of mine. It's just that sometimes it's good to talk. It's so much easier with strangers. They have no preconceived ideas or hidden agendas.'

'I'm sorry,' Judith said, feeling overwhelmed.

'Claude is damaged goods.' He looked at her closely as he spoke.

'What happened to his father?'

'He died within two years of Claude's mother.'

'So Claude lost all his family in his teens,' she replied in disbelief.

'They were such a close and happy family, one of those families that seem to have it all. You know what I mean – money, beauty, talent – the lot.'

'Gone, all gone.'

'Almost,' murmured John.

Judith wanted to sculpt the absence and the loss, to give it a physical existence. 'It's an escape,' she said, whispering to herself. Nothing made sense. The only way back for her was to frame a lump of stone to form the concept of loss.

John passed her a cup of coffee. She felt as if Claude had been dismissed, as if grabbing a lump of French bread and smothering it in jam was a kind of consolation.

She turned away at that moment, aware of John's gaze.

'This is a pilgrimage for me,' she said at last.

'I believe that some artists have an almost religious significance for some people,' said John as she turned her head towards him and licked the butter from her lips.

'Waking up here is surreal; it's the beauty.'

'It is indeed the beauty.'

Marie and Claude came in with bowls of yogurt filled with honey and fresh fruit.

'C'est bonne, oui.'

'Oui, oui, Madame. C'est bonne, c'est très, très bonne,' said Claude unexpectedly.

The gaze he threw at Judith touched bone, or so it felt. He walked away into the garden, looking lost and bewildered. John followed him, picked up a tube of orange paint, smelt it, and looked at it.

Now squeeze out some of it,' said Claude.

John did as he was bidden. The huge straw hat he was wearing brought his face into shadow. The sight disturbed Judith, but she had no idea why. 'Now, place that somewhere on the canvas – anywhere,' Claude told him.

John obeyed and heavy lumps of orange appeared. 'Is that okay?' he asked. 'Or is it too thick, like jam?'

'It's not jam. Paint can never be jam. There are some things in this world you just can't do. Painting with jam is one of them.'

'It's just…' began John.

'It's just paint. That's all.'

'Where shall I put it?'

'Wherever you wish,' Claude said. Judith watched the interaction between these two men. It interested her; they were clearly very close.

John put a few blobs on the canvas, and then he added a different colour. He became immersed in trying to match the colours to the sky and the trees.

Claude took a step backwards and watched from a distance. 'You seem a bit uneasy,' he remarked.

'It's nothing, nothing at all,' she replied, becoming involved in her own work, slowly realizing that emotions are mysteries. They emerge without warning, with a life of their own, like colours on a painting.

John wandered away.

She wanted him to stay. She wanted him to know it all.

'Emotions are such strange creatures,' John said eventually on returning to the exact spot where she stood.

'You think they've wandered in uninvited.'

'That's what emotions do. They wander in. It's their nature,' Claude said, looking directly at Judith. 'They don't mean to, but they do.'

'Precisely.' John handed them both a glass of wine as he spoke.

She stared at her own canvas – scarlet, red and black lines running parallel to one another. A ploughed field filled with blood, the furrows overflowed like rivers. Claude said that he could almost smell the blood. All her senses were directing her hand across the canvas.

Judith's picture produced a mood; it changed the dynamic in the gîte. Claude removed himself from the garden, away from the painting, away from the ploughed field filled with blood, away from her. She realized that the painting had taken him somewhere far, far away. It had frightened him.

'Why? Why did you do that?' he asked.

'I don't know.'

Claude fetched one of her paintings that he had examined the night before and placed it next to the one she had done that morning.

'Neither of these paintings is academically correct. They both contain inaccuracies of form, which some might describe as lies, but both of them are truer than literal truth,' he said.

He looked more closely at the painting of the olive trees and the gravestones. Claude said he thought it to be about the relationship between the dead that was highlighted by the relationship between the shades of green. He asked her how many gravestones there were in the picture. It seemed very important to him, and this puzzled Judith.

'A hundred and one,' she replied reluctantly.

'How many shades of green did you mix for this painting?'

'A hundred and one.'

'The different greens reflect the different people and the different lives,' he went on. 'Truth emerges through the colour as much, if not more, than through the form.'

He went on to say that he thought that the painting was glorious. He loved it, or so Judith believed. There was emotion around her painting; it embodied the disturbance caused by the one she'd done that morning.

'I'd like to know more about the life that could inspire such a painting,' said John.

'You know what families are made of...so many shades, so many hues. It's mysterious, isn't it?'

'Every family is different. Have you sisters, brothers?'

'I had a brother. He died before I was born. He was a year old,' she replied.

'Like van Gogh. His mother had a child who died before he was born.'

'Perhaps that's why I'm drawn to him. I do feel a bond with him that I don't feel with other painters. I admire other painters, of course, but it's not the same. With van Gogh, there is a certain empathy.'

She lay down on the lawn in the sun, realizing that paintings evolve, like life, like relationships. You don't know how, or when they will end or what will happen to them. A painting is a journey with a beginning and an end.

Where will this end? she wondered. She conceded that something indefinable had been pushed through or even pushed away. She knew she wanted to stay in France with Claude. The thought of returning to London filled her with dread. The experience was bigger than her being; it had carried her almost out to sea, and she didn't want to return to the shore.

This is going through me. It's taking over from me. It's bigger than me. I'm simply the instrument through which this organic force is passing. This understanding frightened more than mystified her.

'That painting you did this morning... What did you think while you were painting?' John asked quietly as he sat down beside her.

'This whole enterprise is rather frightening. I didn't exactly see it in that light – the greens and the grief, I mean.'

'What about the gravestones? It's inevitable really, don't you think?'

'Graves are about endings. Without endings, there would be no graves. People have to end some time.'

'Green is the colour of spring, and to mix so many different shades is an explosion of life. Despite the gravestones, it's a manifestation of renewal and of hope. You could have named it "Resurrection" don't you think?' John went on.

'Maybe, but it's a kind of haunting,' Judith replied, with a faraway look in her eye.

****

Once back here I set to work again. The brush however falling from my hands and knowing clearly what I wanted. I've painted another three large canvases. They're immense stretches of wheat fields under turbulent skies, and I made a point of trying to express sadness, extreme loneliness. ... I'd almost believe that these canvases will tell you what I can't say in words.

—Vincent van Gogh, July 1890

Judith wondered about this man whose name was Claude. He came to paint, to laugh, to love, but, mostly, to be. He wore colourful shirts made of linen – sometimes red, more often green, occasionally cobalt blue. He floated, rather than walked – his trousers blew in the wind. She felt attuned when he was around – attuned to sunshine, showers, and thunderstorms. Lightning strikes in all the right places; it surges, burning the sky above and, somehow, beyond it. She tried to think, to collect her thoughts, but without success. The realization was not obvious or fast or clear; it just was. She watched him move around; she waited, and she watched. The watching was protective, strong, throbbing, and insistent. It was the movement of the captured; his presence was too direct. She couldn't breathe if he stood too close or laughed too much. She tried so hard to distance herself, but distance was impossible. She was drawn, as if to the light of certainty.

She sought out John. He offered some protection from the inevitable – the moment when we fall into the abyss, for that is what love is. She threw a veil around herself – she covered herself more; she wore longer skirts. From short smocks and painters' shifts, she appeared in skirts that fell to the floor. She tied her hair back as if to assert control where no control was possible. Instead of falling like a thick curtain, it fell in coils and curls around her face. Somehow, these waves settled around her eyes, creating shadows where none had been before. This drew attention to the darkness contained within her soul.

One morning, she joined John for coffee.

'How long have you painted?' he enquired.

'Since I was a small child. Twenty years or thereabouts,' she replied.

'Oh, so you were encouraged – when you were young, I mean. You were encouraged, then, by your parents, I presume?' he went on.

'My mother used to paint. When she was young, she designed fabrics for dresses and that kind of thing.'

'Were you an only child?'

'I told you earlier I had a brother who died before I was born,' Judith replied with thinly disguised irritation.

'Oh yes. Yes, of course. How did he die?'

'I don't know. They never spoke of it.'

'I see,' he replied.

'No, no, you don't see. You don't see at all. Nobody sees,' she said

rapidly.

'Don't they?' he replied, softly stroking his cheek as he spoke.

'No, it's…not mentioned. No one is allowed to…' Her words fell all over the place.

'Mention it?' He spoke directly, looking at her closely.

'No, not…exactly.' His manner disarmed her; he would make her tell him everything. The idea frightened her.

'It must be difficult if it's not mentioned.'

'I don't know,' she replied, looking directly into his eyes.

'What? What don't you know?'

'What happened. The death wasn't discussed, and yet it was what it was all about. Everything, everyone was all about it. We are all about it. That's what my family is all about – it.'

'An identity. It's your family's identity. Is that what you mean?'

'Yes, exactly,' she confided, with unaccustomed certainty. 'Sometimes it's deep; sometimes it's as if it doesn't matter at all.'

'Everything matters.'

'If it didn't matter, then he wouldn't matter. It's like he's torturing us from the grave with this mattering, this massive overwhelming mattering. It's a wound that hurts everything, all the time.'

'The wound that would not heal.'

'My mother's a war zone. It's as though your body is disposable, as though it doesn't matter if it gets thrown around and trampled on. I've always felt like a rag doll – it's what I am, you see. I'm not involved in the mattering.' She spoke rapidly, as if there were no time to draw breath.

'Do you matter?' he asked.

'No one should ever leave without a loving gaze,' Judith replied.   'Painting makes me matter. If I paint, I matter. What I paint about matters. When I paint gravestones, death matters,' she went on.

'Is that why you paint?'

'I paint because I have to. It's the force that drives me.'

'I see that very clearly in your work. Is that why you're attracted to Van Gogh, do you think?' John asked.

'I love his frenzy. It's familiar.'

'Frenzy, did you say?'

'Yes, the way the colour vibrates. It almost dances with…with the light.'

'It has a luminous quality,' he replied.

She felt his warmth fold around her. It gave her a rare feeling of security. 'You are safe.'

Something made her feel uneasy. She wished that he could discover it, uncover it all – but that would disturb the network that was her life. It would be far safer to let it remain buried, like an archaeological dig where nothing is found and yet a lot has been learnt.

Judith's mind suddenly flashed back to the day when she went to the bathroom to find blood-soaked towels. Rivers of blood crossed the floor. There was nothing to dry her hands on, yet she knew that she had to dry them before school or there would be trouble. The next memory fell rapidly without warning – the evening of that terrible crash when her mother had fallen out of the shower. It was as if her head had burst open, releasing the crimson liquid all around. The terror that came with believing she was dead re emerged.

Cleanly and efficiently, she gathered her scattered thoughts together as she had done so many times before. A scarlet blanket had been hurled across the heavens like the sunset she gazed at the sky until darkness fell.

CHAPTER TWO

*I find it hard to bear this thought and even harder to bear
the thought that much dissention and sorrow in our home
may have been caused by me. Should that be the case, then
I wish it were granted to me not to live any more.*

—Vincent van Gogh to Theo van Gogh, August 1879

She watched Claude set up his easel and begin to paint. That
evening, the chrysanthemums grew from nothing.

'Chrysanthemums represent the moon,' Judith murmured.

'I never knew that.'

'It's the element of the mystical that draws me in. Sunflowers
represent the sun; chrysanthemums are associated with the moon.'

'Is that what you believe?' Claude asked.

'Yes.'

'I believe in some kind of interconnection between species. It's
this connection that I call God. He's the glue that holds the universe
together.'

The long brush strokes produced a soft, lean image. Slowly, he
mixed the colours of white, pink, red, and grey, producing a
translucent skin tone. Claude painted on, as the night slipped gently

away, until a female figure with black hair emerged. For hours, Judith watched this metamorphosis.

'It's exquisite,' she whispered.

'Like you.'

They were both afraid to move, in case the spell was broken. But, at last, he laid down his brush, gathered her in his arms, and carried her to bed. He caressed every part of her until he heard the whimpering, the crying; it was only then that he entered her with extraordinary gentleness. She pulled him deep inside and felt the warmth, the heat, and the strength. She held him within her so that he grew huge. She'd never felt anything this large; how much he'd grown. How much more, she wondered, could he expand? Without warning, she screamed and her back arched. She grabbed him, moaning, pleading with him to go deeper and harder. He grasped her throat, kissing her neck as he came inside her. She felt his warm fluid run down her legs, between her thighs, like a thick river, carrying her forward into love, far beyond the immediate, the future or the past.

The morning broke. There had never been such a morning; there never would be such a morning again. It was the beginning of new life. This realization came to both of them as they sipped coffee in the early hours while the sun rose from pink skies. It was a time when laughter came so easily. They danced among the shadow that is dawn. It was not clear, but then, at such times, nothing is clear; for only love is clear, and that brings both its pleasures and its terrors.

How, Judith wondered, am I to keep my gaze away from his face? How am I to keep my arms securely by my side? Will my thoughts be controlled? Will they be under my command? Or will they assume a life of their own? This confusion continued for several days, if not longer – or so it seemed, because such matters belong to the land where time and space are suspended.

What of her hands? Would they stay faithfully attached to the paintbrushes? Or would they perform unbidden actions? She wondered how she would stop them from touching him and how her eyes would examine paint and light when all they saw was him. When he was out of sight, her vision searched him out.

She curled up in her bed as if nothing could be seen, or should be seen, wishing to hide and protect that something that had nourished her and made her feel alive. It was an elemental force that drew her on. The power of it made her shudder; she thought, in those moments, of tornadoes and hurricanes, those natural forces that change lives forever. The events of the past night would change her life forever; she was a part of this man as surely as she was a part of the earth she inhabited. He had grown within her but also around her, and it was necessary to be alone to absorb and process this event. The moisture of her nightgown reminded her of his moisture. His scent lingered on, slicing through any shy, retiring thoughts that she might have entertained – nothing could tarnish this ultimate truth, or so it seemed.

Slowly, quietly, she emerged from bed and entered the shower. The hot water cascaded through her hair and down her back. Motionless, she stood, allowing it to saturate every inch of her body. The rich soap smelt of almonds. She'd saved it for a special occasion. Her best friend had bought it for her last Christmas. It was the only present she remembered and, thus, the only present that mattered. She thought of her friend, who had been there when she'd chosen it that day in Liberty's. Christine had been around for so much of her childhood – she knew the darkness it contained better than almost anyone. Judith wanted that communion that is female friendship. She wanted it now because, in a very real way, she felt afraid.

Will this be the thing that saves me from myself? Will this be my salvation – or will it prove my downfall, my annihilation? she wondered as she massaged the fragrant shampoo into her hair. She remembered clearly the way her mother had tugged mercilessly at her hair and how the tears had smarted in her eyes – but how she had refused to give her the satisfaction of seeing tears. She had known from a young age that her tears of pain gave her mother pleasure, and that was the one thing she vowed never to do – she would never, ever give her pleasure, never make her happy. How could she, after all? What would be the motivation? The tub of hair conditioner was almost beyond reach but not quite. Thick globs of avocado oil fell over her scalp and ran down her back. This held her in some mysterious way; it was the familiar smell that sustained her. All may have changed, but this was still here – the same as ever, the same as before this night, the same as before she walked into that gallery, the same as before she saw him standing there. In such moments, something must remain untouched, unaffected. If not, chaos reigns. The Lord of Misrule lurks at such times; it is familiarity alone that keeps him at bay. The realization dawned on Judith as she dried herself and put on her oldest Armani jeans, bought by her father to celebrate her being accepted into the Royal Academy and the fulfilment of a dream. They reminded her of a time before Claude. They were familiar, they were safe, they were friends, and so she loved them.

Marie arrived to prepare breakfast. Claude painted. Judith realized this was what he did – as aspects of his life changed shape, so his paintings did too. He marked movement in this way. Images came and went. The canvas before him contained the chrysanthemums of the night before, but now there emerged lines of blue around the skyline. His presence disturbed her peace, this peace that passed for concentration.

John asked him questions about van Gogh's preoccupation with cypress trees. They both needed a distraction, and he provided it.

Judith thought immediately of her own preoccupation with olive trees and of the similarity between the two obsessions. Van Gogh saw a distinguished green in the strange shapes, just as she did. This understanding made her eyes restless. They were neither still nor focused, but moved around in their own orbs exactly as they saw fit. She moved away from him and spent the rest of the day with just canvas and an easel for company.

She discovered a small shrub; it was fairly humble, not striking in any way, and yet it touched her. It was so easy for her to discover the inherent energy in this plant. This strange image came to life; she felt the life force as she painted it.

Concentration deserted her when Claude came over. He took hold of her face and suffused it with the warmth and the strength of his kisses.

'How are you getting on?' he asked eventually.

'I'm not sure, really. Different visions come into my mind – not the usual ones; it's all rather unreal,' she replied. Images fell into her mind, which was an untidy room with hidden objects, objects that had been covered with white dust sheets.

The weather got warmer and warmer. Lethargy and love cohabited. Judith thought that it was probably what people referred to as happiness.

John found a large mushroom and began to paint it. The fungus grew quickly and took over the entire canvas until nothing else existed. Judith wondered if this was his intention, or whether it was an unconscious inclination to change the emphasis of the painting, to change the mushroom from the innocent to the malign. She wanted to reach out and touch it.

The intense heat melted inspiration. What they wanted was to swim and stare. Conversation slowed. Claude and Judith lay like lizards, soaking in the sun and in each other. Their torpid limbs fell around, utterly changed by such a small thing as climate. It dictated everything – the way they dressed and moved; the times they slept; what they ate; and, indeed, what they didn't eat.

Judith realized that the subject of van Gogh's insanity excited and disturbed Claude in equal measure. His eyes held a look of both fear and fascination when he spoke of it, and she wondered why it had such a hold over him. Why was he so obsessed with this man? It seemed to her that his instinctive impression remained unchanged no matter how often he returned to the subject. He was utterly convinced that it was Gauguin's abandonment that led van Gogh to cut off his ear and that the pain of this loss drove him insane.

She came to believe that Claude's extraordinary empathy with the painter was reflected in his carnal desire for her. It fuelled it in some way that she didn't entirely understand. All she knew was that it surrounded every single cell, every corpuscle, and every part of him. It manifested itself most strongly during moments of intimacy, those moments when they wandered into sun-drenched fields where sunflowers abounded – the fields where Van Gogh had painted. Claude tethered her in his arms. There was no possibility of escape as he thrust into her. All she could do was surrender to his power. At those times, she felt the presence of the dead painter emerging from the scorched earth on which she lay.

One day, he told Judith about a woman in England whom he had been with for eight years. This triggered her initial dread of returning to London. Her anxiety manifested itself in many different ways; she ate less, she slept little, and she desired Claude more and more. She pleaded with him to remain in France and not to return to England. She suggested a garret somewhere, anywhere, where they could hide away and paint. All she wanted was to be with him away from London. She wouldn't have minded very much where they went and for how long, just as long as they were alone and together.

Claude disagreed. He wanted to go home and resume his life, but with Judith.

The day of departure inevitably dawned. They got onto the ferry together, sat on the deck, and watched the sea and the sun resplendent in a cloudless sky. There were, of course, things they could have said about the beauty of the waves as they washed around the huge boat or about the seagulls cawing overhead, but it wasn't the time for words. There was something in his kiss, in his grasp. He literally lifted Judith off the ground and held her against his mouth. She felt blurry, as if he were suspending her in mid-air merely by the force of his kiss. She pulled away from him, almost falling backwards. They stood facing each other breathlessly. She was filled with desire for him, a desire to bite into his flesh, a primal hunger for his body. His mouth filled her mouth. He was steadfast and strong.

CHAPTER THREE

'Fuck art! That's all I can say,' Annabel shouted so that everyone in the cafe could hear. 'Would you believe it? He's gone to France. I shan't see him for at least three weeks, probably more,' she said, staring into her sister's face.

'I've come to see you because you asked me to, but if you're going to behave like this... We've been over and over this so many times before,' Ruth replied impatiently.

'I've a good mind to take this promotion they've offered me in Handford. I have to make up my mind.'

'Tell me more.'

'Well, they want me to go down there for six months to sort out the budget deficit they have at the hospital.' Annabel looked around her, appreciating at last the wonderful aroma of freshly roasted coffee beans. She loved this place in Westbourne Grove because the cake, as well as the coffee, was always perfect. Just being in this environment lifted her mood. It was her favourite haunt. She met her sister Ruth regularly. They were very close, despite the difference in their brains and looks. Annabel knew her sister was pretty; she had lovely blonde hair that reflected the light no matter what and a dainty size ten figure. Annabel was envious, but she realized that she had something that was far more valuable – she had brains. This asset was her trump card, and she used it. At seventeen she'd gone to university in London and had been awarded a first in pure mathematics by the time she was twenty. She went on to study statistics in health service management for her MA. Now, at the tender age of thirty-two, she'd made it and took pride in her achievements. Her great weakness, she knew, was Claude.

She'd rescued him. She'd supported him through the dark days of his grief, the days and the nights when he'd clung to her for succour and support. She'd given him her all – that was the problem.

'I think you should take this offer. Go to Handford. Forget about him,' Ruth said.

'I'm going,' Annabel replied softly as tears ran down her face.

'You have to accept it. He's not going to marry you, or he'd have done it by now, or at least proposed.'

'He's had a charmed life.'

'Hardly. he lost his whole family because of that bloody accident.'

'You know what I mean. Inheriting that house when he was so young,' Annabel said bitterly.

'You've also been blessed. I'd love to have your brains. You didn't even have to work all that hard for your first. I struggled with A levels and failed, while you got straight A grades across the board. For a while, I hated you.'

'You never told me that before.'

'I don't now. I will if you don't take this job in Handford.'

'I'll take it. I'll tell them tomorrow that I'll go.'

'In the meantime, take my afternoon appointment at Aveda. Go and have a facial and a hair-do. It'll make you feel so much better.'

'Are you sure?'

'Yes, I'm very, very sure. Talk to the therapist; she'll advise you.'

'I suppose I could brighten up my dreary hair, couldn't I? My face needs a complete overhaul, but I don't think anything on earth could improve it.'

'Don't be silly. Your face is fine. It's a kind face, and your eyes are a lovely green.'

'But my hair is the colour of a carrot, and it's all curly and messy,' she muttered.

Ruth reached across the table and hugged her sister. 'Go on. Off you go. Have a bit of pampering on me.'

****

While walking along the road, Annabel thought about her parents and how odd they were, living up in the Hebrides. She'd never been happy up there with them. This was the place she loved – dirty, smelly wonderful London. What, she asked herself, will Handford be like? Bloody hard work, she knew that. Yet, financially, she would be richly rewarded. She'd earned it. She gazed into one or two dress shops.

Maybe, she thought, *I should have a bit of retail therapy instead of going to Aveda.* Having promised her sister, though, she felt bound to go. 'It might work,' she reasoned. 'They just might be able to make me look a bit better.'

She walked through the door and her mood immediately lifted; it was so soothing. A therapist sat down next to her.

'Is there anything you can do with me, or am I beyond redemption?' she asked.

'You're very striking, but that's to your advantage. What would you like me to change? How can I help you?'

'My hair and of course my face. That goes without saying. Can you make it look less like a bunch of carrots?'

The therapist smiled at her before she spoke. 'Well, I could tone down your hair if you wish. How would you feel about copper?'

'I'd love that. If you could turn it copper, that would be wonderful. And get rid of some curls. What about my face? Can you improve that at all, or do you think it's a lost cause?'

'I think a bit of tender loving care is what it needs right now. I could certainly give it that.'

So Annabel placed herself in the hands of this excellent woman and fell under the spell of the essential oils that were massaged into her face. She relaxed and came to understand the futility of her life with Claude. *Love*, she came to realize, *is not given because it is deserved.*

I'll go away. I'll accept this promotion. It'll be a challenge. I won't have time to think about Claude. I'll be far too busy.

****

Handford was, in many ways, a strange place. Annabel arrived from London to begin her new life, the life she and her sister had mapped out for her. The hospital was small and modern. It pained her to say it, but she fitted in. She fitted in because it was as it was. She liked what she found, and what she found was secure. It was so different from St Mary's, Praid Street, where she had both worked and trained in financial management.

The first day, she met a lot of people and was introduced to the computer system. She spent most of the first afternoon getting to grips with the geography of the hospital complex.

In the evening, she threw off her shoes and fell in front of the TV. She had rented a flat on the outskirts of the city. It was okay – not great, but okay. She thought about Claude before she went to sleep. This was not how she had imagined her life would be – but it was what it was. She dreamt of cats and laser machines. When she woke up, tears fell down her cheeks as she wrapped herself in her duvet. Sleep didn't return to her that night, so she woke exhausted and only just managed to get to the hospital in time.

She heard a knock on her office door.

'Come in,' she said as a tall brown-haired gentleman entered.

'Good morning. My name's Simon, and I'm the regional manager. It's so good that you've come here. We got wonderful references from London. I'd like to show you around.'

'Thank you,' she replied. Her reputation had preceded her, and she knew it.

'Would you like coffee?' he enquired.

'Yes, thank you. That would be good.'

The coffee duly arrived.

'London's a long way from Handford. What made you decide to come?'

'My family has connections with the county. My grandmother lived near Handford for twenty-five years. She was a midwife. She married a doctor.'

'Did you visit her then?'

'Yes, sometimes.'

'So you feel at home already?'

'I suppose I do.'

'Good. Let's walk round, shall we?'

The two walked around the hospital. As she did so, Annabel thought her decision to take this opportunity was the sensible thing to do. The wards were modern. Some of them were mixed-sex, which was something that Annabel felt strongly about, she was opposed to them. She spoke to most of the ward sisters and a few nurses. She knew they were probably thinking, *Oh, no. Not another bloody manager.*

Well, she was worth her money; she knew that. And soon she would prove it. She made mental notes as she walked – notes on cleanliness, on ward numbers, on what staff were doing, on how many there were. All these details came automatically into her mind.

The long tour came to an end at last. She and Simon had lunch in the canteen. The food could be improved and certainly the coffee, she noted.

'Well, first impressions?' enquired Simon as they arrived in the office.

'Lots to think about. That's my impression.'

'Tomorrow, you'll be introduced to the consultants.'

'I'll be eyed with suspicion then.'

'And fear…'

The evening arrived and Annabel decided to visit the cathedral. She hadn't been there for years, but there were happy memories as she walked, thoughts of Claude flooded her mind. She missed him so much. Love for him had seized her heart and made it ill.

Bloody men, bloody men, she thought as she sat alone in the chancel. One or two of the male fraternity threw a glance her way as she left. Annabel knew she was adequate – her looks were adequate, her figure was adequate, her personality was adequate. Only her brain was extraordinary. On returning to her flat, she opened the fridge door, poured Chardonnay into her glass, and relaxed as thoughts about the past day entered her mind. The hospital was fine. It would never set the world on fire. No great discoveries would emerge from within its walls, not like the research that St Mary's, Praid Street, produced. But then, that was one of the great medical centres of the world. Handford was quite well equipped, with X-ray equipment, at any rate. This pleased her. She liked equipment, and she thought that, if she could find ways to reduce costs – and thereby the deficit – she would be able to free up money for more equipment that would, eventually, save the lives of the population of Handford. She was motivated by a desire to save lives and had considered studying medicine, but her natural talent lay with mathematics, and she understood the importance of playing to one's strengths and making the most of natural talent.

She understood very clearly that the deficit in the hospital's budget was putting lives at risk; that much was immediately clear. There was even talk of reducing the number of consultant posts. This idea appalled Annabel, and she was determined to find alternatives. No reduction in cleaners or doctors – she would find cuts elsewhere.

She washed her hair, wrapped herself up in bath towels, and sat in front of the TV. At last, the luxury of soaps, without guilt. She indulged in them all that night – *Coronation Street, Eastenders, Hollyoaks...* She loved the misery of other people's lives because it made her forget her own. She had a TV dinner – tuna and pasta bake. It was fine. Annabel was content. Eventually, she went off to bed and slept soundly until her alarm woke her the next morning.

I think I'll change my car, she thought as she sipped her early morning tea and munched her way through a slice of toast and marmalade. *It must accommodate my new image of independent womanhood. After all, that's what I am – an independent, successful woman.*

She dressed with great care. The day would be long and hot. Eventually, she selected a grey cotton-silk trouser suit that she had bought at East and black stilettos, which always gave her a sense of power. She felt confident, and as she drove past Steels garage, she glanced at the array of cars on display, making a mental note to call in there on Saturday. This would give her something to look forward to, she reasoned to herself.

She arrived at the hospital and went swiftly to her office, reviewed the previous day, and worked on her computer until lunchtime.

In the afternoon, she met a few individual consultants, alongside whom she would work for the foreseeable future.

An effort would be made to stay within budget, but the demands were increasing. She listened to what they said, and the situation was not as she as not as she had at first envisaged it. There was more waste in the hospital than she had realized. The deficit problems needed to be addressed as a matter of urgency. There would be redundancies; it was inevitable. The consultant from the intensive therapy unit was the final meeting of the day and the most difficult meeting so far. Annabel suggested scrapping one ITU bed, which the consultant took as a personal insult. He argued that such a move would, inevitably, cost lives. She said that the deficit made change inevitable. And, anyway, much of the time ITU nurses could not be found so agency nurses had to be brought in at great cost, a cost the trust could quite simply not afford. The consultant, Christopher Graham, was furious and said that cuts had to be made elsewhere, and that was all there was to it.

She thought about it as she drove across Handford in heavy traffic. The journey seemed as if it would never end. She wished she had at least some motivation to exercise. If she had, it would all be okay. She'd feel better if she were more in control of her life. But it wasn't there; it just wasn't. It was horrible. She hated herself at these moments. Any normal healthy person would have sprinted or jogged from the hospital to her flat – not Annabel. Claude had bought her membership at an exclusive London club one Christmas. The club had a gym and a swimming pool, but she never went. She loathed it and told him so. It was, she said, full of people with perfect bodies, the kind of body that she would never have.

On arriving back at her flat, she poured a glass of Chardonnay and sat down to phone her sister.

'Hello? Oh, hello, Ruth. It's me, Annabel. I'm trying to get my head round this new job.'

'Sorry. I'm sorry,' Ruth replied.

'It's okay. I'm having a bit of a panic day.'

'I see.'

'I don't know exactly…'

'I was worried about you after our last meeting, very worried. You were so unhappy.'

'Yes.'

'It'll be okay.'

'Why, why, why?'

'I was really very worried about you. I thought you were heading for a breakdown.'

Annabel drained the Chardonnay and saw that the bottle was empty. She slammed the phone down and wandered into the bedroom, tripping over her tights on the way. When she at last turned off the TV, sleep evaded her. During the night, she tossed and turned, this way and that, as thoughts tumbled through her mind. She wanted to find that place, that peaceful place, but it was not to be.

What I wouldn't give to be in Claude's bed now, she mused.

The morning arrived. Work took on an intensity that she relished. A few consultants arrived, and she tried to reassure them as best she could. She was asking for tenders from cleaning firms to see if there were more options to consider in this area, though somehow she doubted it. Work cleansed her of emotion; she had no time to feel but merely to think of solutions to the deficit. It was work that had saved her once before, and it was proving her saviour once again.

She returned to her flat in the evening, feeling raw. Yet another TV dinner, this time macaroni and cheese, awaited her and then another round of TV soaps, followed by another bath. She cried herself to sleep. When morning came, she noticed her wrinkles. They were caused, she guessed, by nothing more than the force of gravity. She pushed her face around to see if she could improve the situation but without success.

I want to be beautiful and wise, but I'm not. I'm efficient, she thought sadly.

Today was the day she would meet with the senior nurses and see what they had to contribute, if anything.

The meeting was long and arduous. They insisted that it would be impossible to cut nurses' hours without compromising patient safety.

'Why won't you even look at my proposals?' she asked.

'We're the ones with knowledge and experience. We don't need to find fresh ways round this problem. We need all the nurses we can get, and more, just to keep things as they are,' the senior nurse replied.

'I'll be doing time and motion studies to see if there are improvements that could be made,' Annabel said.

'I'm sure you will. I'm sure you will,' said one nurse, with venom in her voice.

'Look, I've simply been brought in to look at possible changes that might help to reduce the deficit.'

In the middle of the afternoon, the phone rang. It was her sister wanting to come down and see her.

'I'm busy right now. Ring me this evening.'

The day came to a rather miserable end, with more department heads phoning to complain about possible cuts. Annabel got into her car exhausted once again and drove home.

She felt lost. She was beginning to hate this job and this rather dreary city. She put her feet up on the table and threw her shoes across the room. At least St Mary's had been interesting. She missed her friends, Claude, and all that went with him. The next three months were spoken for. She had to stay; there was no alternative. At this point, the phone rang. It was her sister.

'Hello,' Annabel muttered.

'Hi, it's me. How are you?'

Annabel didn't reply at once. 'Okay. I'm here, and that's how it is,' she said eventually.

'Why don't I come down and see you? It would be good, really good. You have a spare room in that flat, haven't you?'

'Yes, and a sofa bed. When are you coming?'

'Friday evening.'

'No, don't come until Saturday. I'll be so exhausted on Friday I won't be fit for anything,' Annabel replied.

'Is it that awful?'

'I don't want to talk about it,' said Annabel and put the phone down yet again.

She got out yet another TV dinner from the fridge, poured herself a large glass of Chardonnay, and settled down on the sofa for another night of soaps.

'It's okay. I'm okay,' she said, trying to convince herself that this was true. At 11 p.m., she ran herself a bath. As she soaked, she contemplated immersing her head in the warm water and leaving it there. On balance, she decided it might be more unpleasant than not doing so and eventually retired to her bed.

She wondered what the psychiatrist would be like, the one she was due to meet in the morning. He was in charge of the drug and alcohol unit; addiction was his specialty. Annabel had already earmarked his department for cuts. She thought a ridiculous sum of money was being spent on this area. These were her final thoughts as she drifted into sleep.

****

Annabel made enquires about Geoffrey Dove the next day, prior to their meeting. She found out that he had just returned from his annual holiday in India and that he was relatively young for a senior consultant – only about forty. Her secretary warned her that he had a reputation for being fiercely protective of his department and his staff.

The day was hot. She felt anxious about the meeting, which had been scheduled for that afternoon. What she had to do, she knew, was get the measure of the man and, by listening to him discussing his department and the work that he did, elicit his strengths and weaknesses. From that, she could devise a strategy that would enable her to achieve her objective. She prepared herself for the inevitable battles that lay ahead. It was going to be war, and it was almost certainly going to be bloody; the mentally ill always took resources.

Why, she wondered to herself, do we have to spend so much money on addiction services? Surely personal willpower should be enough – and, of course, common sense. She began to wonder if she was addicted to Claude. She missed him so much and wished to be with him.

Care in the community. That's what I'll suggest, she decided. She wondered why the drug addicts couldn't be cared for in the community. She wrote down her thoughts on the computer.

The appointed time came, and Annabel heard a knock on the door. She was carrying a half-drunk cup of coffee. She smiled and lit up the air around her with it it was a technique she had learnt during her management training. Geoffrey was startled, but he stretched out his hand.

'I'm Dr Dove, the senior psychiatric consultant here.'

'I'm Annabel Griffiths, the finance manager.'

'I know. Coffee would be excellent.' This was a command that she obeyed.

'Psychiatry – now that is something I've been considering,' she said slowly.

'Yes, well I suppose it would be…an easy target.'

'I hope I don't think that way. Your caseload is heavy. You have a lot of service users.'

'Of course I do. I always have.'

'I want us to think imaginatively about…' she began, drawing him in with her eyes.

'Reducing numbers,' Geoffrey muttered.

'What are your main objectives, your professional priorities?'

'To provide my patients with the highest possible level of support and to empower them towards independent living,' he replied.

'I agree. Independent living must be the priority.' She watched closely as he shifted uncomfortably in his chair, knowing what this meant.

'There are many of my clients for whom this will never be a realistic possibility. Supported housing in the community would shift funding away from the NHS and away from this hospital I know.

However there will be other expenses if unsuitable clients are placed in the community and very, very real risks. Risk assessments have already been carried out on all my service users. We update them regularly.'

'The budget for the unit is very high. It appears to be something of a rolling door. The same patients reappear again and again. Why is that?' Annabel asked.

'The people who return again and again usually have severe psychotic episodes induced by delirium tremens. Some are drug-resistant. It's important that the client, his or her family, and society in general are kept safe until the crisis is resolved,' he replied.

'It seems that even on the addiction unit, after the six-week treatment programme, clients are returning again and again. This surely needs to be reviewed. Hundreds of thousands are spent on these programmes. Are they value for money if the clients return again and again?'

'Many of our clients don't return,' Geoffrey retorted.

'According to the data, 60 per cent return – more than once.'

'I've only returned from holiday today, so I haven't checked the figures.'

'This is an area where cuts need to be made.'

There was a quiet certainty in her voice that disturbed him. 'You are certain of both your facts and your judgment, aren't you?'

'The data has come from your own psychiatric department,' she said. 'Medicine, and psychiatry in particular, is not an exact science.'

'I understand that; of course I do. The human mind is inexplicable in a way that financial deficits are not.'

'Clients return for a multitude of reasons.'

'I don't question that – not for a moment.'

She saw him looking at her. She knew what she ought to do, what she needed to do and what she was being paid to do. And, yet, despite it all, there was something getting in the way. She didn't quite know what it was. There was no weakness in her argument. She was, she knew, a master of her craft and, as a result, had managed to make him doubt his own position.

'I've been employed by the trust to sort out the deficit problem. That's my remit.' The man's discomfort was becoming ever more apparent.

'My department is always the one that is targeted. Why can't you leave it alone? Just once, leave it alone,' he replied at last.

'All departments are having to make savings. Even ITU is to lose one bed. If you don't agree to my suggestion of a reduction in readmissions on the addiction unit, I shall have to consider recommending to the trust that you lose a consultant.'

Annabel saw the rage on his face.

'Society will pay in another way if addiction facilities are cut. There'll be more crime and more crowded prisons,' he replied, getting up and wandering around the room.

'You're right, but that isn't my concern. I'm not a social worker, and neither, incidentally, are you. We both have to do the best we can with the facilities available. There is a limited amount of money. The trust needs to find ways reduce the deficit.'

'I'll think about the options you've presented me with. I'll get back to you. If I lose a consultant, that will affect the care of psychosis, bringing inevitable dangers.'

Annabel waited patiently. She enjoyed his presence, despite the difficulties, and she felt sorry for him. Despite his obvious humanity, he would lose the argument, and the budget for the addiction unit would be cut.

****

She returned to her flat exhausted as usual. She thought about the day that had passed and the conversation that afternoon. The attraction of her job was that it was so difficult. There were always wars to fight, people to placate and to argue with – often simultaneously. She had chosen health economics for her MA because it interested her and she thought it was worthwhile, but at times like this, it overwhelmed her. Reaching for the bottle of Chardonnay that sat on the table in the kitchen, she poured herself a large glass.

It's warm and stale, like me, she thought.

The phone rang. It was Ruth.

'Hello.'

'Hi,' replied Annabel.

'Is it all right if I come over on Saturday and stay for the weekend?' 'Yes, but I'm busy in the morning.'

'What are you doing?'

'Car browsing and then a facial.'

'What sort of facial?'

'Anti-wrinkle, anti-ageing, anti-sagging – you name it, that's what I'm having.'

'Oh, the complete works.'

'Pretty much. I'll be through about one.' 'I'll have lunch on the way.'

'Yes, that's a good idea.' 'See you tomorrow.'

****

The following morning, Annabel wandered across the road to Steels Garage where she found a divine Fiat 500 with only 10,000 miles on the clock. It was black with a white leather interior and a hi-fi system to die for. It was, quite simply, love at first sight – chic and sassy, as only Italian cars can be.

Well, she thought, *if I can't have the man I love, at least I can have the car I love.*

The deal was complete by noon, and she walked out of the showroom a happy lady.

Her sister arrived and screamed with delight at the sight of the Fiat.

'Oh, it's gorgeous!' exclaimed Ruth.

'Isn't it just,' replied Annabel. 'Come on up.'

They went up the stairs to her flat, which was modern and soulless.

She had yet to put her mark on it. Annabel knew she was clever, but she didn't have an artistic idea in her head.

'I'll make some coffee.'

'How are you getting on with your new job?'

'It's okay. It bought me the car. Who am I to complain?'

'What do you want from me? What do you want to hear?'

'Weren't they weird, Mum and Dad? They had so little – just moods and feelings. They're the worst things, and yet they wallowed in them, always examining them and asking why they felt what they felt. When they weren't doing that, they were watching birds.'

'Don't you think they ever longed for retail therapy?' Annabel replied. She grabbed her handbag and marched out of the flat.

Ruth laughed at her sister's ridiculous pronouncement and walked down the stairs after her.

The afternoon wore on. The heat impacted their mood. Annabel bought a tailored silk trouser suit for work and a pair of black patent heels – the power dresser extraordinaire.

They settled eventually in a pub garden and ordered a large jug of Pimm's, which arrived brimming with ice, strawberries, and mint.

'What did you think of him as a person?' asked Annabel.

'Claude, you mean?'

'Yes. As an outsider, what did you think?'

'I thought he was weird, but then, artists tend to be. He was very, very intense. Utterly absorbed in his work. I never believed he loved you. That was the most difficult part of the whole damned business. I knew he was screwed up with grief and remorse – that was obvious – but it was so damned difficult because he was so complicated. But you had to find out for yourself.'

'I never knew you saw him in that way. I don't understand.'

'You understand things that most people will never understand, and yet you can't see what is clear and obvious to most people,' Ruth said slowly between sips of Pimm's.

'What don't I see?'

'How screwed up, how neurotic he was in so many ways.'

'I don't know what you mean.'

'Take it from me, Annabel, that man will never make you or anyone else happy. You're well rid of him.'

The sun and the Pimm's made Annabel drowsy. She and her sister wandered home together, yet she felt utterly alone.

The phone rang as soon as they got in.

Ruth picked it up.

'May I speak to…oh no, never mind.'

'Do you want to speak to Annabel?'

'Well…yes.'

'Hold on.'

'Annabel, there's someone on the phone who wants to speak to you,' said Ruth, passing the phone over.

'Hello.'

'Oh, hello. I know this is unprofessional, but I was wondering if you…could come to lunch tomorrow. I thought, since the weather is so wonderful at the moment, we could eat in the garden.'

Annabel recognized the voice at once.

'Well, thank you. It is a bit unusual but tempting. It would be odd.' 'Life is a bit odd sometimes.'

'That's certainly true. What the hell – I'd love to come.'

'Noon, say? I'll come and pick you up.'

'Yes.' She gave him the address.

'Goodbye.'

'Who on earth was that?' asked Ruth the moment Annabel put the phone down.

'A work colleague. Well, it's a bit…unusual, unorthodox, to say the least. But it could be beneficial, you see.'

'Go on.'

'He's the senior psychiatrist at Handford. We'll talk about funding issues away from the hospital. He'll feel less threatened.'

'I believe in fate,' said Ruth, smiling to herself.

'You always jump the gun, don't you?' Annabel said angrily.

'I'm going to make some coffee and then, sister dear, you can tell me everything.'

'It's just lunch; that's all. You don't understand. I have to use various strategies to obtain objectives. It's called politics, and it's never ever straightforward.'

'We're going to spend the rest of the evening making you divine.'

'We are. Of course we are,' replied Annabel, laughing at last.

'It's so good to see you laugh – so good. You haven't laughed for months and months.'

Much of the evening was spent in the bathroom. While Annabel stretched out in the bath, in all her size-fourteen glory, Ruth scrubbed her back and used the opportunity to glean more information.

'Go on. Tell me.'

'He's a psychiatrist. Don't make more of this than there is. He simply wants to expose my weaknesses. Then he'll know how to win the battle.'

'How intriguing.'

'Not at all. It can be productive to meet in relaxed surroundings.'

'Why?'

'People feel less defensive, less threatened, when they're on their own territory,' Annabel said impatiently as she emerged from the bath. It was, she realized, pretty hopeless to try to explain the complexity of her work to her sister.

In the meantime, Ruth rustled up a large salad, some new potatoes, and cold ham, which she had discovered nestling in the fridge – almost hidden behind the TV dinners.

'You're almost – but not quite – the perfect sister!' Annabel exclaimed when she saw the feast her sister had prepared.

'I can't believe that. But I do try.'

The main topic of conversation throughout the meal was Claude.   'Is it okay, about Claude?' asked Ruth gently.

'It is as it is. I have to get on with it. I feel uneasy about him; that's the problem. He walks across my mind as if he owns it.'

'Is it okay here, I mean?'

'It's okay. It's better now that you're here. The job is difficult, but it's a challenge.'

'Maybe tomorrow will prove—'

'It's just lunch in the country on a gorgeous summer's day.'

About midnight, Annabel went to bed. She tossed and turned.

Thoughts of Claude in France disturbed her. She dreamt of a court of law that was impossible for her to leave. Strange birds sat in the public gallery and waited for her. There were bars outside the court; she was imprisoned. She woke up and thought she heard a sound, but there was no one there. Clasping the duvet around her, she fell into a deep, dreamless sleep.

****

In the morning, she reasoned that these disturbed dreams were a result of overwork, nothing more. It had happened before, earlier in her life when she was in the Hebrides with her parents. But these night-time apparitions disappeared in their own time and in their own season. It had at the time no logic. A doctor had concluded that she was suffering from a depressive illness and was floundering around trying to deal with it. Depression she knew to be a disorder of mood, and yet it contained an air of mystery. Those who experienced it found it so overwhelming as to be beyond expression. She realized that her mother found it totally incomprehensible, and so did her sister Ruth. They'd never spoken about it except to say that things would improve when she went to university on the mainland – which they did, and it had never returned until now.

Why now? she wondered. She had tried so hard to make things work, but it was all to no avail. She couldn't get Claude to commit. In fact, it was worse than that; she knew she was losing him. This admission caused tears to well up in her eyes. They ran down her face. And, as she wiped them away, she understood how powerless she was to alter the situation.

In order to comfort herself, she made tea and toast, smothering it with thick raspberry jam. Then she put on her make-up. The tactile sensation that this provided gave her some comfort. Ruth styled her hair. She was good with hair. Before she married, she had trained at a top London salon for three years. At the time, Annabel had been amazed that it could take three years to train to be a hairdresser. *What,* she had wondered, *could there possibly be to learn?*

She saw his car outside the window at noon. They drove off into the depths of the Herefordshire countryside and eventually arrived at a large black-and-white house. It was clearly old; the walls were a bit crooked and the roof newly thatched.

It was immediately clear to Annabel that Geoffrey loved this place and was anxious to show it off. He showed her round the garden and the huge apple orchard beyond. A big dog bounded out to meet them as Geoffrey bought some delicious food out into the sun.

'Why did you take this job? It must be hell,' he said. 'Depends on your definition of hell, I suppose.'

'What's yours?'

'Being trapped in a situation or a place that you can't escape from,' replied Annabel.

'I see.'

'What's your personal definition of hell?'

'To lose someone you truly love.'

'Has that...happened?

'Yes. When I was twenty-five, a women I was engaged to walked out on me. I've no idea why. She just left.'

'It's so painful, isn't it? And it's as if they don't care at all. Maybe they don't,' she said, thinking about her own pain, acknowledging to herself how much she needed Claude, despite everything.

'Yes, that's it. I threw myself into my work, let out this house for three years, and went to the Institute of Psychiatry and then the Jungian Institute, where I studied for my fellowship.'

'I wondered how you rose to be senior psychiatrist at such a young age.' 'Well now you know. I'd like to discuss the addiction clinic that I've been running for the past ten years, and I thought this would be an ideal opportunity to explain my work and why it's so important. You see, the support we provide is a lifeline for many families. It's a support that can't be duplicated anywhere else.'

It seemed to Annabel that this man was truly committed to maintaining this facility, no matter what it cost. 'Are you saying it's a unique facility?' she asked.

'In this county it is. It serves the West Midlands.'

'It's not my decision to make. The trust will decide. I'm only here in an advisory capacity. I've been asked to identify clearly where cuts could be made with minimum impact on human life. That's my remit; that's what I've been asked to do and what I've agreed to do. It's in my job description, so there's no question about it, I'm afraid.'

The afternoon brought further discussions around psychiatry, both its dangers and its challenges. Annabel asked him why he chose to specialize in it. He said it was because people fascinated him. She saw the interest herself and found his enthusiasm contagious; before she knew where she was, she found herself caught up in his world. They drank jugs of home-made lemonade mixed with Pimm's and lay on hammocks in the orchard. Slowly but surely, Annabel relaxed, as the sun warmed her face. She knew that he thought he'd achieved what he'd set out to achieve, that he'd weakened her resolve. But then, he didn't know Annabel at all.

****

Judith opened the door of her flat and checked the knives. They were still there where she'd left them. Her father had not discovered their hiding place. She brought in her paints and brushes, placing them in the studio. How long, she wondered, would it be? When she thought about her mother, there was always this dread, and then darkness followed. What would happen when Claude found out? She was annoyed with herself for thinking in this way after such a life-affirming week. The truth was that such thoughts were never far away. Dreams and memories emerged—days spent in cupboards, blood-soaked bathrooms, clearing up the red congealed mess that resulted from her headlong descent through mirrors or down stairs. These images invaded her mind. They burrowed away inside her head like maggots.

In an attempt to blot them out, she walked into her bedroom and found some paper. She drew Claude with the edge of her pencil. As the figure emerged on the paper, it terrified her. Claude wouldn't want her once he knew the truth. She placed the paper into the back of a drawer so that it wouldn't be seen by anyone.

She went back outside and brought in more things from the car – tubes; tubs of paint; and many things that could not be found at home, like soap from Provence and big bags of lavender to put under her pillow at night or in between her clothes. She'd bought French sheets from a market, and she placed them on her bed. White sheets went well with shrouds; her nightdresses always reached to the floor. She wouldn't have it any other way.

There was a sense of unease that she could not dislodge. Why, oh why, had Claude insisted they return to London? He kept on saying that they had to return. They could have run away and lived in a garret somewhere and just painted, like van Gogh and Gauguin did. Her father would have prevented them from starving; she knew that. Judith's needs were simple. She could, or so she believed, live on very little. No matter how many times she'd told him that she wanted to be lost with him in France, in Europe, anywhere – even suggesting living in Paris – nothing had worked. He'd insisted on returning home to London.

So much had happened in France that could never be changed. Despite this, Claude knew his place in the world. He knew that he belonged in his house, in his home, and that was where he wanted to be. Nothing she said could disturb this feeling. She understood it – envied it even – but for her, it was unimaginable. Swans on the pond and the people nuzzling together for warmth on cold winter days had been a feature of his life and of hers, like underground trains and bright red buses. But their connections to these things were different.

Joy and love, which now pervaded every step, could, she imagined, change and be replaced by something else. She had discovered something that was new, and it had to be assimilated; this frightened her. She began to think of ways of keeping her dreadful secret. Mr Rochester in Jane Eyre suddenly entered her head. She vividly remembered the way that he'd tried to keep his mad wife a secret from

Jane. She too could pretend that her mother didn't exist, that she was dead. She could tell Claude that she'd died of cancer.

Would her father go along with the lie? That was the question. She thought of phoning him. Was there anything he wouldn't do for her? She asked herself this question over and over again until she thought she would go mad.

The phone calls would have to stop now, right now – no more police, no more custodial sentences, no more visits to the ghastly prisons or the psychiatric units. It had to end. Judith realized that, if she threw away her phone, her mother would simply get in a taxi and come round without either warning or hesitation. Claude might be there.

France was so gorgeous. She'd never ever been so happy. She would never be so happy again.

Why couldn't we have stayed forever? She'd never have found us. I'd have escaped forever from her chaos, her destruction. Here, I'm caught in a web.

She went to bed and dreamt that night of insects in the banks. When she woke up, she remembered the times when they refused to give her mother any more money. She'd shouted at the cashiers and thrown empty bottles at them. The police had then arrived and taken her away.

This issue with her mother was not the only problem. There were others. Judith was not domesticated. The state of the floor in the kitchen simply could not be described. She was a slut.

What, she wondered, *would Claude think if he could see me now?* Hot tears ran down her face. She got out the dusters, but it felt as if she were cleaning herself. Why should she clean herself? She wanted to start cutting as her thoughts spiralled out of control. There was no problem with bandaging them up. She had jumpers, sweaters, T-shirts, and dresses that all had long, loose sleeves so that she could easily hide the cuts and the bandages. Judith was meticulous in this regard. She never cut too low or too long. He held her wrist, it was sore. Seeing at once the line and the cut, he took it to his mouth and kissed the scar. He pushed her sleeve up. She tried to pull her away in embarrassment but he held it more tightly.

She lay in bed that night and thought that she could change, but the times when she'd tried to change had always ended in failure. However, she knew that she would have to change if she was to keep Claude. She could live on bread and jam for a week or two and get a cleaner. The trouble was, they never stayed. They just wouldn't stay. One morning, and they were gone. One cleaner had reported her to environmental health. They'd sent someone round, but the representative just mumbled about it and left.

It was the cockroaches that really did it. She'd tried to get rid of them, but they didn't want to leave. Why should they, after all? It was warm. There was something to eat most, if not all, of the time, so naturally they were content. One day, she placed several on a plate in the microwave. But it was no use – it didn't kill them. Now she was unsure that she wanted them killed. They had chosen her, and Judith was unused to being chosen. Claude had chosen her, the Royal Academy had chosen her, and the cockroaches had chosen her – that was about it. Friends disappeared after a trip to the flat. Even cats weren't keen.

She soon abandoned the dusting, made some scrambled eggs, and started to paint. As she did so, the phone rang. It was Claude.

'I was missing you.'

'I'm painting right now,' she replied, trying to control the panic in her voice.

'What are you painting?'

'Chaos – that's what I'm painting.'

'Tell me more.'

'There's no more to tell.'

'You seem distant,' he replied.

'No. I'm concentrating; that's all.'

'Can I see you?'

'It's not easy, just now.'

'Please.'

'I'll sort something out and ring you back,' she murmured.

'Okay.'

She hung up and felt panic rising. She was going to lose him. She knew that. As soon as he saw the flat, he'd be gone. Getting out her mobile phone, she looked up the number of the cleaning agency.

'Look, can you send someone over tomorrow? It's urgent.'

'How many hours? It's fifteen pounds an hour.'

'Oh God, six hours. I want the whole place cleaned, except the studio.' 'Yes, there is someone I could send out for six hours.'

'Thank God for that – 10 a.m. start. I'll be out for the day. Ten until four or five, depending on whether or not they want a lunch break.'

'Fine. The address is as before? I presume you haven't moved?'

'No, I haven't moved. I'll be here to let her in.'

She sighed with relief. It was going to be okay. She'd live on bread and cheese and have a cleaner. The cockroaches went into hiding behind the sink, reluctantly. But they were, as always, so uncooperative. It was very unlikely that they would stay there until the cleaner came. And, of course, they didn't.

Claude agreed to meet her. It had all turned out fine. She wanted to see him again as soon as she could and without any restrictions.

Judith began to paint, and there emerged, after a long and protracted encounter with the canvas, a central theme, which involved time. The inevitable olive tree emerged. Among its branches were faces that hung upside down and sideways, cut into portions like oranges. Facial segments fell through the branches. Judith emerged from the studio at midnight, lay on her bed, and slept.

She woke at eight, made tea. The cleaner arrived at ten as arranged. She was a pleasant, intelligent woman who didn't judge Judith at all. A secure feeling emerged that said, *This is okay, you know.* This woman would remove the cleaning problem. She said she lived just round the corner and would keep things spick and span. She was sick of working for the agency and wanted something that was close and regular. She said she loved a challenge, and Judith's flat provided just that.

Her father would protect her. He always had done, in his way, and would continue to do so. The thought of him made her feel safe, but where was he?

She phoned him repeatedly in the weeks that followed. He owned the flat where she lived and kept an eye on her. When she allowed it, he came to visit her. She wondered where he was. He didn't answer his phone. Occasionally, her mother picked it up. The sound of her voice took Judith back to places she didn't want to go. She loathed the sound of her mother's voice, the sight of her – even the smell of her.

Weeks went by, and at the end of July, Judith had still heard nothing from her father It made her uneasy. Had something happened to them? Where was he? What had happened?

At the same time, Claude's passion filled her life, and he couldn't get enough of her. He stayed with her in her newly cleaned place. Before he entered her, his body would tremble and shake as if there were a battle raging within him. It was almost as if a new energy had filled him and somehow enlarged him and the space he occupied. His gait was stronger.

Despite this, what Judith wanted was her father. Despite everything, despite the love, the passion, and the laughter, she wanted her father. Where was he? That was what she wanted to know.

The emails she sent him came back. They were always exactly the same: 'Glad you're back. Glad France was wonderful. Very busy at present. Delighted that things have worked out so well with the cleaner. Don't call round – I won't be in. Dad.'

It was not easy when it was like that. He was so strong and so strange with his thick black hair and his unmistakably Jewish face. She wished he'd phone, but he didn't. One day, on the very last day of July, Judith decided to go and visit him anyway.

What do I have to lose? she reasoned, walking toward her parents' house. His car wasn't there. She delved deep into the recesses of her handbag, and there was the key. She opened the door and saw that the hall was a mess, with brightly coloured coats and handbags strewn all over the place.

It was at that moment she saw her mother lying on the floor, unconscious. This was not unusual. She'd been like this so many times before. Judith's childhood had been littered with scenes like this for as long as she could remember. The sight of her mother sickened her. She felt tired, nauseous, and dizzy.

How long have I wanted you out of my life? How many times, when friends called, have you made me cringe with embarrassment? The apothecary of memory opened every drawer in her mind that morning. Recollections preceded feelings, many of which had been hidden for years. Perhaps it was the passion, the intensity of her desire for Claude that opened closed pathways and released her inner darkness.

'Wake up! For God's sake wake up!' she shouted. There was no response.

Her mind returned to the moments in childhood, when, standing over her mother, she'd shouted exactly the same words. Images flooded through her mind, where they tumbled and jostled for position. She looked at her mother lying on the floor in front of her, stared at her. She pushed down a moan of sorrow, and then released it.

Dimly, as if through a glass, Judith knew that this was the moment she had waited for all her life. The idea emerged from nowhere, sealing her own fate as surely as it sealed her mother's. The large pool of vomit that lay on the floor provided her chance for revenge. Slowly and deliberately, she turned her mother's head towards the foul fluid, pushing it into the vomit. She watched as the liquid entered her mother's nose and mouth. The taste of revenge melted on her tongue.

She thought of her beloved Frumps and what her mother had done to him with that knife on that dark day so many years ago. It was the most delicious moment of her life; it was sweeter than she'd ever imagined it could be. Her mother attempted to lift her head. She looked Judith in the eye and tried to push her away, but she was too weak. She was no match for her daughter. There was no contest. She struck out, but this only served to intensify Judith's resolve. Grasping hold of her mother's hair, she pushed her face down into the vomit once again and kept it there. The breathing became shallower and shallower, until it ceased altogether.

There had been no planning, no malice or forethought. Fate had presented Judith with the chance to commit the perfect murder, and she'd taken it. Entering the kitchen, she found a cloth and wiped the floor where she had sat, and then the front door handle and all the surfaces she'd touched.

Could death really be so easy? Could life be extinguished with so little effort?

Slowly opening the door and entering the street, she found it quiet and relatively empty. Her mobile rang. She ignored it, walking instead towards Kensington Gardens, up into the orangery and past St James's Palace. What was taking place within Judith was unfamiliar. She crossed the park and wandered along by the side of Kensington Gore and past the Albert Memorial and eventually arrived at Knightsbridge. She entered Harvey Nichols and ordered coffee but couldn't drink it.

The hairdressing department of Harvey Nichols was upstairs. Judith took the lift. A woman approached her and asked how she could be of assistance.

Her reply was definite. 'I want it all cut off – all of it. I don't want any of it to remain.'

'It's lovely. I could do a restyle if that——'

'I want it all chopped off,' she repeated.

'I'm sorry, I can't do that, I cannot do as you ask. I have a duty as a creative stylist."

'It has to be altered…' Her fingers hesitated, and then they trembled. 'I understand. You want a complete change,' the woman replied. Judith walked to the washbasin, realizing she was shaking. A young girl massaged her head. She loved the hot water flowing around her. Suddenly, without warning, it was over. The water stopped flowing.

She sat upright in the chair as her hair was cut. The black waves hit the floor. The stylist looked at her closely as she cut. The scissors felt cold in the nape of her neck. Slowly, a heavy dark fringe emerged that emphasized her eyes, which became larger and more prominent. The mirror in front of Judith revealed her mother's face staring back at her. A memory crossed her mind of the day her mother had shut her in the cupboard under the stairs. It had been so dark in there. She could feel the blackness inside her head now reflected in the darkness of her hair; memories of the hunger pains coupled with the fear that she would never get out, memories of shouting, 'I promise I'll be good! I'll never be naughty again!' She couldn't get out; she just couldn't get out.

Judith thought that, if she physically moved, thoughts would shift and memories would dissolve. So she paid and quickly walked downstairs to the cosmetic department, where she tried on various lipsticks – vermilion, red, and poppy. What she wanted was something dark. She found a lipstick called 'rouge noir'. It was the deepest red she'd ever seen. This triggered another memory, of when her mother had hit her until her nose bled. She knew immediately that this lipstick was the colour of that blood. She bought it without hesitation, along with the matching nail varnish. The assistant asked her if she would like to see the eye make-up for the new season. The colour palate she brought could best be described as gothic; the mascara was a dense black velvet, as was the matching eyeliner. The assistant applied it to her heavy lashes and outlined her dark eyes with it.

Judith looked in the mirror and said, 'It's perfect – the colour of midnight.'

'No,' the woman replied, 'it's darker than night; it's the darkest black I've ever seen. It suits you perfectly. It's identical to the colour of your hair.'

'I shall wear it always because it is, as you say, darker than night.' Alabaster foundation and ivory face powder completed the look.

'The queen of the night,' the woman replied.

Judith looked away, hurriedly paid, and left the shop.

It was raining outside, but it didn't matter. She trudged through the wet streets as the rain ran down her back, through her hair, and down her face. Buses were out of bounds – there were people in buses, ordinary people. Judith was not one of them. If she'd learnt one thing that afternoon, it was that she was no longer as others were.

She could never ever be ordinary again.

She no longer belonged to any species.

This realization dawned on her as she hurried through the rain-soaked streets of London. At the bottom of Kensington Church Street, a large red bus stopped. Someone she knew spotted her, jumped off, and approached her. It was John, the man she'd met in Provence. He took off his enormous raincoat, threw it round her, and stared for several seconds.

'This rain is torrential!' he exclaimed.

'It's complicated,' she replied, as if to a stranger.

And, in a way, he was a stranger. Everyone was now a stranger. She was a stranger in a foreign land.

'Let me take you home,' he said.

She didn't resist. He hailed a taxi that passed by. They got in, and it took them speedily to his flat on Moscow Road. The flat was huge and old. It had a musty air and a strong odour of beeswax. The place was lined with bookcases, many containing leather-bound volumes, that reached to the ceiling. The floor was covered with Indian rugs with symbols of Hindu gods woven in various shades of gold. The leather sofa looked hundreds of years old; horsehair stuck out of it.

John went into a linen cupboard to search for some dry clothes for her. He emerged with a shirt and a pair of soft trousers, which were far, far too large. Her arms and legs vanished beneath the dark grey material.

'I'm going to make tea. You wander around and see if you can find something more suitable,' he said.

She went into the bathroom, ran the bath, got in, and lay back, immersing her whole head in the water and staying there until she thought her lungs would explode. She scrubbed and scrubbed her skin with the loofah and lay down again, only to see her mother's face reflected in the water. She watched the drips from the taps and heard John calling her. On the back of the door hung exactly what she needed – a green towelling gown, ancient and generous.

The coils of her hair were gone. The length was gone. Her eyes were so dark she winced at the sight of her own face.

Is this me? she wondered.

John looked at her. 'What's wrong?' he asked softly.

'Wrong? Wrong? What do you mean? Nothing's wrong.'

'There is something wrong,' he insisted.

'Suppose I tell you. What then?' she replied, feeling the need to unburden herself.

'I'll listen. That's all I can promise.'

'I want to go home now.' She couldn't trust herself not to tell him what she'd done. Everything became vague; there was nothing for her to hold on to.

'Do you remember what happened?'

'Nothing.'

'I think you should stay with me for a while. I'll go and make some tea. I have some scones and strawberry jam.'

Judith's thoughts were all jumbled up. It was as though she were unable to negotiate her way from one thought to the next.

'You'll tell Claude if I stay here, won't you?'

'Not if you don't want me to, but why don't you want him to know? I could say you're ill and are resting here for a few days.'

She couldn't move but sat there in a trance, unable to make decisions.

How would she ensure her own survival without telling them that she'd found her mother when she arrived at the house? Then Claude would be moving. Nothing would change. All would be fine. On the other hand, if she told the truth, the fabric that was her life would fall apart. The threads would unravel. Judith didn't want that – that was the one thing she knew for certain. She wanted her life to go on as before.

Why should I be punished? she thought. I've been punished already. My beloved Frumps was punished.

If she went home to her flat, people wouldn't ask questions. On the other hand, if she stayed with John, people would ask questions. It would be simple to go home. Yet, there was a fear of being alone. She wanted the reassurance that John and his home could provide. At that moment, her mobile phone rang and she answered it.

'Hello? Dad… No, I'm not at home now.' She put the phone away at the very bottom of her bag. If it was out of sight, it would be out of mind. Yet, for some reason, she didn't turn it off.

'We all need help sometimes – never forget that,' John said as he emerged from the kitchen with tea and scones.

Judith picked up the cup he handed her and felt the hot liquid surging down her throat. Her hands were shaking.

'Where have you been?' he demanded.

'I had my hair cut. It was too long, much too long.'

'I see,' he replied slowly.

The phone went again. It was her father.

'Can I come round and see you?' he asked, with a note of hesitation in his voice.

'Yes, do that,' she replied.

Judith suddenly got dressed and left the flat without a word to John. She felt afraid of all the people in the street. Every step took forever. Her feet felt like lumps of stone – cold, heavy, and unyielding, as if they were detached from her being. At times, she had to place them deliberately on the pavement. It was as if they did not want to move.

When she arrived home, she looked round her flat and found it both clean and tidy, smelling of lavender furniture polish.

It's too good for me. I shouldn't be here, she thought.

No, you shouldn't. You damn well shouldn't. Her mother's voice reverberated through her head.

Judith curled up in a ball on the bed and waited for her father.

Hours later, the doorbell went. And there he was, standing there, this man she loved above all others. 'I'm so pleased to see you,' he said as they sat down on the soft sofa.

She looked at him, this lovely man, so tall with black hair that was receding a very little at the front. He possessed great presence, having trained at RADA when he was young. He had a voice that he could modulate and change at will and an ability to be someone other than himself, as and when life and circumstance demanded it. He was handsome; there was no doubt in her mind about that. Why, she wondered, had he let it all go for so long? Why had he allowed this to happen? Why hadn't he protected her? He'd failed her. He'd failed to protect her. He'd employed people to care for her, but it never worked. They never stayed because her mother's behaviour drove them all away. Why, she wondered, couldn't her mother have stayed in the addiction units? Why hadn't any of them worked?

'Tell me about the day you met her,' Judith murmured.

'I'd been invited to a party held by an old school friend, not long after I left RADA in 1980. The party was dull beyond endurance, but there was one spark of life. She was there in a brilliant yellow dress,' he mused.

She watched him, but nothing was clear. It all seemed like a blur, as if she were seeing him through a fog. For the first time in her life, there was space, dark space. Tears fell down his cheek.

'You love her even now, don't you?'

'Love is not given because it's deserved,' he replied.

'Why then? Why is it given?'

'Love falls'

'I don't understand. I thought you hated her. Truly, I did.' 'I pitied her.'

'You tried to help her. I know you did.'

'Nothing worked. It all started after Harry died. She was inconsolable all the time, and I didn't spend enough time at home with her. Your grandfather died suddenly, and I had to take over the business. There was so much to learn. I didn't have time for her.'

She watched him, but his words fell away. They made no sense. Her hand trembled as she poured the drinks into the glass, spilling some on the carpet.

'Judith, I have something to tell you,' he murmured. 'I'm afraid your mother died this morning.

'I don't know how it happened. I went out – I had to. I had appointments to meet surveyors. She was drunk when I left, but then, she often is, as you know. I have a business to run, a living to make – you know that – people to meet. I tried. I tried, but after the death of Harry, she changed. She changed so completely. It was then it started – the drinking I mean. She just never got over it – losing her baby boy, her first baby. I wanted to help, but she was inconsolable, utterly inconsolable. The grief took her away from everything – from me…from life.'

There were no spaces between his words; he spoke so rapidly. She listened to him, knowing that, in spite of everything, he still loved her mother. 'I didn't know you loved her.'

'No, neither did I. There was pity. I pitied her after Harry died. Even now I pity her. The death of that tiny little boy caused a brainstorm, a howling tempest from which she never recovered,' he said sadly.

'I'm sorry. I'm so sorry, Dad,' Judith whispered. Suddenly, there was nothing to hold on to. It was as if her mind were lost. The only impression she had at that moment was her father's forlorn face. She latched onto it, reached for it in the abyss that had become herself.

Her father gazed. It seemed as though he were boring deep into her skull, attempting to discover the secret within.

'Are you…okay?' he said at last.

'I don't know what that is – not now.'

She moved away from him, towards the window, and saw her mother's face reflected in the glass. She pulled the curtains in an effort to escape the image. Yet it remained imprinted on her mind.

'What is a mother?' she murmured, mostly, if not entirely, to herself, thinking about the intensity, the vengeance, and the horror of it. She thought of the bloody beginning, the emerging into life, the blood, the mess, the separation, and the power of the umbilical, for good or ill.

She heard the doorbell ring. She opened the door. Claude was standing there in front of her.

'This is my father, Sam,' Judith announced.

'It's not the best time,' Sam replied.

She felt bewildered. There was no connection to either of these men.

The connection to them both had gone, vanished, and not a trace of it remained.

'My mother died today.'

'What? What did you say?' Claude said.

'My mother died today.'

Claude looked at her.

'It was sudden…her death, I mean,' she stammered.

'How did she die?'

'Drink killed he'

'The devil killed her.'

'No, Judith, grief killed her' Sam replied.

'Go away. Don't come back here, ever,' Judith said, looking at both men. 'You don't know what you're saying,' Sam whispered.

'How could you love her? I didn't know you loved her. I thought you tolerated her.'

'We don't love people because they're nice or because they're kind.' 'Why then?'

'Love falls,' Sam replied.

Judith wanted to be alone. She felt unsafe. Why should she feel safe or secure, having moved out of that zone? She couldn't return to it, for this was a foreign land. It was unknown territory. She felt like a mountaineer feels, seeking the next safe ledge to put her foot on. Claude looked at her. The rope that had held them together had snapped. She had fallen, and he couldn't catch her as she hurtled into the void.

The two men left.

She slept for twenty-four hours and, on waking, made thick bacon sandwiches and poured ketchup on them, stuffing them into her mouth before stumbling around her house, feeling disoriented from the night before. Was it all a dream, she wondered? But as soon as she saw her image in the mirror, she knew this not to be the case.

Claude phoned and told her that he was due to give a series of lectures on van Gogh's devotion to Japanese art. It was open to the public, and he wondered if she would like to go with him. How extraordinary it seemed to her that he would want her mixing with art collectors. Why didn't he know that people wouldn't want her there?

'Why do you want me mixing with people?' she asked.

'Judith, don't be so silly. Of course I want you to be there.' 'I don't understand what you're saying I'm so cold.'

CHAPTER FOUR

The night found Sam sitting on a bench in the centre of a small private park. The moon was full, and it seemed to this man, on this night, that it had centred itself on him, and him alone. He felt selected, the centre of the stage, the spotlight. He remembered the day he'd met his wife, Virginia, twenty-five years ago when he was just nineteen. In that moment when he first saw her, he was drawn, as if by a magnet. She fell into his life. She had been in it ever since – until today.

He thought about the death that had precipitated her descent. He had denied it for a long time. It remained a mystery that he could never comprehend. It was as if her mind had been dominated by some archaic disconnection. Sometimes she was lucid in the mornings, but as the day wore on, a murkiness gathered around her, bringing with it both panic and dislocation. It was as if her thought processes were engulfed by a toxic tide that obliterated everything but the desire for alcohol. It was, he recalled, like observing someone in self-possessed agony, which was connected to suffocation and also to drowning. Sometimes, after Harry's death, she would fall onto the bed and lie there for hours gazing at the ceiling, in a trance.

Anyone entering this private park might have mistaken Sam for a huge bird; his arms and upper body were swathed in a dark silk cloak, which he wore often on hot summer evenings. He'd acquired it originally from the vaults of one theatre or another – the spoils not of war, but of drama. Thick black hair fell just beneath his ears. The moonlight illuminated the blackness of his eyes and the luminosity of his skin. He was a slender man with long lean limbs. He shone like a huge bird. He stood up and circled the bench on which he had been sitting, grasping his hands as he walked and then releasing them. Round and round he went.

Why, he wondered, do I feel as I do now, at this time and in this moment? I didn't love her so very much. There was life before her. There will be life after she's gone. I'll get over it. Of course I will. I'll feel passion again before my life…

He knew that he'd never again run his hands over her, as if caressing a stone that enclosed the salt of eternal oceans or the light of a star. The truth was that she was ugly in every way that a person can be ugly. Her cruelty was hideous. And yet, despite it all, he loved her. She desecrated everything and everyone she touched, even the daughter he adored. Yet still, he loved her. Inevitably though, there were also times when he detested her. He remembered the nights when he would return home to find her drunk and abusive. Memory is a mere pharmacy, a chemical laboratory in which our groping hand may come to rest – now on a sedative drug, now on a dangerous poison, now on a sunset.

Sam returned to the bench, put his head in his hands, and wept. He wept for himself alone. It was a selfish weeping. It did not cover him in glory. Now, as the moonlight shone on him, his soul was exposed for all to see. The universe gazed on him and found him wretched.

How, he wondered, *could I have allowed this to happen? If I hadn't gone out that morning, she would still be alive.*

Guilt became his that night. This was a guilt that had lain softly over consciousness for years, but tonight it rose up within him like a fever. He wanted to put it back to sleep, but now that it had woken, it poured its poison over his grief and produced a very particular toxin that many would call despair.

Dawn approached. And as it did so, Sam gathered up his cloak and wandered back to his home. He opened the door into the hallway where he had discovered his wife the morning before. He remembered sitting beside her, touching her, and feeling the cold, cold forehead. She'd gone, and yet, physically, she was there. He could see her, touch her, but her essence was gone; that part of her that made her unique, different from every other living being had gone.

He moved into the kitchen, made a pot of coffee and sat down to drink it. He thought about the birth of his son, Harry, in 1990. He remembered the joy he'd felt when he'd first seen him in Virginia's arms. Harry had one finger holding onto his mother's index finger. All was as it should be. She smiled, and friends arrived later to wet the baby's head. Champagne flowed amid the joy and the laughter.

Now, here he was in this kitchen, alone. He looked around at the room his wife had planned all those years ago. He liked it because it was familiar. The cupboards, soft green and white, created a sense of space. The kitchen window looked out onto a garden full of flowers. Steps led down to it. He could see Judith in his mind's eye, sitting as he read her the stories that she loved. Stories about Pooh and Piglet had been her particular favourite. He remembered how she'd snuggled up to him for comfort, how the books had given her at least some solace before the next drunken tirade. It was, he realized, all right for him. He could always escape on the pretext of work. And so he had, leaving Judith alone with her mother. How often she had screamed at him, 'Daddy, don't go! Please, please don't leave me!'

He always, always went. He left her there. He stayed away for as long as he could. Why did he do that? he wondered. Was it because he'd been so young? He had been just twenty-three when Judith was born. He wondered as he sat there in the kitchen that afternoon, and he didn't know. He'd never known. There had been remorse, especially when he returned and found her in some dark room or, worst of all, in the cellar, hungry and cold. She would hug him with such joy when he reappeared, and they would cook something delicious and comforting together.

He thought about the vast sums of money he'd spent over the years for Virginia to go into rehabilitation units. He'd employed people, so many people – nannies and au pairs – to take care of Judith, which was what Virginia had pleaded with him to do. Many, if not most, of his friends had advised him to send her away to school he was essentially selfish, and he knew it. He loved his daughter, and therefore, he wanted her to stay with him. He loved his wife too and felt sympathy for her, no matter what.

If only Harry hadn't died. Why had Harry died? No one really knew the answer to that question, and now that his wife was dead no one ever would. Sam sat alone in the kitchen and thought of the little boy's tiny fingers that used to grasp his own and his smile – or maybe it was a burp. You never could tell with Harry. He was such a funny little chap.

I will be dependent on her and on no other even if I could I should not want to be independent on her. But she has loved her another her thoughts are always in the past and her conscience seems to bother her even at the thought of a possible new love., but there is a saying and you know it that one must love, then unlove and then love again. I saw that she was always thinking of the past and buried herself within it with devotion. I thought, though I respect the feeling and the thought she was always thinking of the past and buried herself within it, then I thought though I respect the feeling and the thought and though that deep grief of hers moves me, yet I think there is a fatalism in it, so it must not weaken my heart, but I must be resolute and strong like a steel blade.

—Vincent van Gogh,

CHAPTER FIVE

Annabel wasn't quite certain whether she loved the colour of early September at Ferney House as much as she loved the colour of summer. The truth was she loved it all. The Sunday meals in the garden of Geoffrey's house had become a regular weekly joy. September had brought so much sunshine.

'I'm going to be away next month, for a few days late October. From the twenty-first to the thirtieth to be precise.'

'Where are you going?' Annabel asked.

'I'm going to a seminar at the Jungian Institute in Switzerland. I'm giving a paper.'

'Didn't you say you'd trained there?'

'Yes. I spent four years there after my engagement ended so abruptly. I went when I was twenty-six. I returned to England when I was thirty. It was the thing that saved me from myself. It took my career in a particular direction and deepened and expanded me in a thousand ways.'

Annabel poured herself another glass of Pimm's, thinking carefully about what he'd said and the kind of man he was. She felt out of her depth. This was not the first time she'd felt this way, especially when faced with deeply personal issues that clashed with her own experiences, or mirrored them. She too ran away when personal issues became overwhelming, which was why, of course, she'd accepted the job in Hereford.

'I feel a bit lost. Tell me about Jung.'

'Would you like to come with me?' Geoffrey replied.

This time, just for once, I'm going to be distant, she thought.

She wasn't in love with him. She knew that. That spark, that magic was far, far away – for both of them. This was simply a pleasant interlude. It was never going to be more than a relaxing comforting cocoon. That was not love. Love was many things – comfortable was not one of them. It was never going to be more this.

It's not worth risking my career for, or my professional judgement for that matter, she decided. She knew that her decision regarding psychiatric services was made, and if she continued with this pleasure, she would be expected to make compromises. One of her main recommendations to the trust would, inevitably, involve a reduction in addiction services. This association with Geoffrey anaesthetized her for a time, removing the memory of Claude. Here, at Ferney House, the air hummed. Flies, bees, gnats, grasshoppers, butterflies, and beetles were all there, leaping around in the foliage, living their individual lives in harmony. It produced a realization in her that there was so much life in every particle of the world and in her own being. This was health, she knew. Geoffrey gave her a spiritual awareness; it seemed to be part of his very nature.

'I don't think I can go on with this, with you. I'm not in love with you, though I enjoy your company,' she said, feeling confused.

His response was to make coffee and take it into the lounge where the ceiling was a mass of old oak beams, which had been there for centuries. The back wall was covered with a large tapestry. The colours were gorgeous.

'I wish it was winter,' she said.

'Winter?'

'If it were winter, there would be less life around us.'

They sat together but there was an absence. She felt uncomfortable, ill at ease, and so she made an excuse to leave. 'I'm working tomorrow. I have a meeting with the trust all day. I need to sleep.'

Annabel dragged herself away feeling a little bruised. There were times when it was like that. It took some of her away, like a kind of vanishing, and then she had to have time to find her way back. She wondered if this was why his fiancée had left him. He was too much. Claude had been very different. Annabel realized that she was not loved. She had wanted to be loved by Claude, but she was not. She wanted to be loved by her father, but she was not.

Daddy, you bastard, we're through, she thought while driving along the colourful leafy lanes. It came into her mind that afternoon. She didn't understand why, but it was there, both unbidden and unwanted – a bitter hatred that left her both exposed and vulnerable.

She got back to her flat in Hereford. It wasn't home. It had never been home, and it never would be. Geoffrey wasn't home. He never would be. A black depression hit her as she opened the door. It was as if a sledgehammer had lodged itself in the deepest recesses of her brain. And it was triggered, she realized, by this single thought that had somehow emerged into consciousness during her drive home from Ferney House. She dreaded the thought of the meeting tomorrow. She got into bed and howled into the night and into the early morning light.

****

Jung had changed him, had made him see, know, and appreciate the value of the individual. Every patient, every person had value because they were unique. There could be no replicas and no replacements. A particular interest of his was that of the undiscovered self. He believed that, in cases of latent insanity, where there is some psychic understanding, individual understanding is required. He learnt during his Jungian training that, at its most fundamental level, mental illness is characterized by a disunity of the personality. Conversely, mental health is manifested by unity. He believed this disunity to be caused, essentially, by repressed feelings that lodge themselves in the unconscious and become inaccessible. The more inaccessible they become, the more neurotic the person becomes.

Geoffrey's conventional psychiatric training emphasized different facets of mental disturbance. The medical model was the springboard from which he jumped. It was the part of his knowledge that got him through. His understanding of neural anatomy was considerable, since he had studied neurophysiology at the Bethlem and Maudsley Trust.

However, most importantly, he did not believe that the brain was the mind. He was convinced that the brain was the creator of the mind, just as instruments in an orchestra are not the music, but the music cannot exist without them. The orchestra is much more than the sum of its parts, and so it was with the human brain. What the orchestra produces is music; what the brain produces is mind.

Geoffrey was fascinated by neural networks and the plasticity of these networks – the way some networks could be shut down and new ones could be laid down and formed throughout the life of the individual. The basic structure of the brain consists of billions of nerve cells, neural networks, dendrites and axions. He knew this to be the architecture of the brain and, thus, the foundation on which the mind was built.

He spent the rest of that evening considering these matters and reading works by Jung in preparation for the week or so he intended to spend at the institute. He read about the psychoanalytical ideas as applied to delusions and hallucinations. As always, he was fascinated. There were, of course, the inevitable comparisons with religion and mythology and the links between them. Geoffrey had always been convinced that all the great ideas in history, religion, science, philosophy, and ethics could be attributed to a consciousness that we all share – what Jung called the collective unconscious.

He conceded that many of his Jungian ideas were not acceptable to many of his associates, but this did not trouble him in the least. In fact, he enjoyed being considered mildly eccentric. He enjoyed discussing dream states with his neurotic clients and knowing that this provided valuable insights into their conditions. He understood them better. They talked to him easily. They trusted him. This added so much to his work.

He was always aware that, if his engagement had not fallen through, he would never have gone to the Jungian Institute. He had been, at that time, desperate to escape from the world. He'd inherited enough money from his grandmother to fund the venture, and so he'd let Ferney House and gone. Switzerland he'd found extraordinarily beautiful. The mountains had provided splendid opportunities for climbing, an activity he'd pursued at amateur level since he was at school.

There was no doubt about it, Geoffrey was a deep – some might say profound – thinker, a man who had the capacity to reduce the suffering of the mentally ill very significantly.

CHAPTER SIX

Judith sat in her studio, and an image appeared in her mind, which she transferred onto the canvas. She wanted, at one level, to paint the familiar olive trees, but it was as if they had disappeared from her internal landscape. Instead, what appeared on this canvas was her mother's face. She stared at the image and thought, *I don't want to paint you. I want to forget that you ever existed – that you were, at any time, a part of my life.* She picked up the paintbrush and covered the canvas with a grey wash before leaving the studio, closing the door behind her.

She knew that her father would call round later to see her, but she didn't feel close to him. She didn't feel close to anyone. Her mother's intrusion, her constant presence, prevented that. What was it that she wanted? Why couldn't she leave her in peace? Feelings, she realized, were not just formless floods of emotion that washed over us. They were lasting attitudes that had a logic and a structure of their very own.

Suddenly, in the midst of her reverie, the doorbell rang. It was her father. She walked out into the kitchen, and he followed behind her, watching her every move. Once, not so very long ago, when he looked at her in that way, she would immediately open herself to him, allowing him to see her innermost thoughts. She did not let anyone else see her like that. He could pollinate her with a look or a gesture or, indeed, with his mere presence. Today, she was gone from him; she was no longer his.

'Well then…'

'Yes?'

The conversation jolted to a close, as is inevitable when there is a shift

that at least one party does not understand. Judith wanted him to go.

'What do you want?' her father asked impatiently. 'Nothing.'

'Nothing? I think…'

'I don't care what you think,' she replied.

She let him out and felt the most extraordinary relief. She waited until his car was out of sight, went into her studio, picked up her brushes, and began to paint. The canvas filled slowly with shapes and dark shadows. What emerged was like nothing she had ever painted before; it was the image of a head. She filled the eye sockets with tiny birds' nests and then she painted a second head, similar to the first except that the nose was a beak. It looked half-human and half-bird, the skull filled with brightly coloured feathers. The jaw emerged slowly, becoming uneven and craggy like a coastal path. She felt the presence of Cornwall as she scraped the skin with her palette knife and added little tiny flecks of white and grey. The mouth was slow to conceive, not impossible – not exactly – just very difficult.

She thought about it, and as she did so, memories of the holiday she'd taken with her mother when she was seven years old filled her mind – the walk they'd taken along the coastline and the emphasis her mother had placed on achieving goals. She remembered so well seeing the other children playing in the sand, making sand castles – but not her. She had to climb rocks and go into deep dark caves, to find the tiny crustaceans that lived inside and around the rocks. While her mother attended to the crustaceans, Judith would sing about them; she would give them little funerals. These funerals took on an importance for her mother that Judith never understood. It had all seemed mysterious, mystical even. It was something to do with the mouth. As she looked at the painting in front of her, her lips began to ache and her back to arch.

You are mine, more now than ever. She heard her mother's voice inside her head. Nausea, waves of fear, and anxiety threatened to overwhelm her, yet she sat as close to it as she could.

Claude phoned later. 'Do you think I could come round?' he asked. 'I'm painting at the moment.'

Judith replaced the receiver and considered throwing her mobile away. Instead, she put it in the bin, filled her glass with whisky, and returned to her painting. There were so many images in her mind's eye that she had no need of outsiders. Here, she was locked away from everyone and everything. There existed a sense of alienation and dislocation whenever she was around people.

Claude called round a couple of days later. Judith felt his gaze burning into her. She was convinced that he knew what she had done.

Why, she wondered, does he pretend he doesn't know? How much does he know?

He walked into her studio, saw the canvas, and gasped. He grabbed hold of her and forced her to gaze at it.

'This is…like some sort of carbuncle. I saw your father the other day and he, he…'

'You know nothing about art or about me,' she murmured.

'What? You like this?' Claude shouted as he attempted to wrestle the canvas down from the easel.

'It's mine, for Christ's sake! It's mine! What the hell do you think you're doing? I can paint whatever I like.'

'You've destroyed everything.'

'Get out! Get out!'

'This painting is not you. It's not your style. I don't know the person who painted it. It's not you.'

'It's my self-portrait.'

Claude just gazed at her and then at the canvas and back again. She could see the pain in his face. She wanted him to leave. She needed to be rid of him so that she could be alone with her painting. This uninvited presence was unendurable. Her feelings were as unforeseen and unusual as an accident, as some hideous accident that had occurred in the region of her heart. Love had been removed, as if by a scalpel in some operating theatre.

'Why can't you just leave me alone? Leave me alone,' she pleaded.

'I love you.' And so he stayed, trying to settle himself on the sofa and relax.

'You're much better off without me. Believe it,' she said.

'Do you remember John, the man who was with us in France?' he replied.

Judith didn't reply. She sat and said nothing.

'I've known him all my life. He was a friend of my father's, he wouldn't have made it through without him. I believe you need help. John might be the person.'

Judith didn't answer, but she did remember the afternoon she'd spent with him on that fateful day. There are days, big days – the day you're born, the day you're baptized, the first day of school, the day of your first period, the day you're accepted at the Royal Academy, and finally, the day you become a murderess…

How, she wondered, could anyone ever help her with that?

'No one can help me – ever.'

'I don't accept that, and I never will. I just want John to help you find yourself again – that artist, that wonderful artist who searched for and discovered one hundred and one shades of green.'

'Just go, and remember me that way,' she said.

Claude left John's card on the table, by the phone, and let himself out. On the opposite side of the street, he saw Judith's father arriving in his car.

'Hello, Claude.'

'I've left a card on the table…a friend of my father's who may be able to help Judith. Goodbye, Sam. Goodbye and good luck.'

'I'd…' Sam muttered.

Claude left quickly and spent the rest of the evening at the Sun in Splendour.

Judith's irritation increased when her father arrived. The painting seemed to have taken a further hold on her mind. She didn't seem able to destroy it. Why had it such a hold on her? Why couldn't she let go of it? She'd seen something in that painting that she didn't want to see. She was trying to erase the present from her mind. This mind was altered. It produced hideous images. She tried to reconnect to work she'd done before, but all to no avail.

Painting became her sanctuary. She scrutinized it in minute detail. The work on the canvas became the centre of her life, the purpose of her existence.

CHAPTER SEVEN

'Geoffrey, are you going to Switzerland, to the Jungian conference?'

Geoffrey picked up the message on his answer phone and returned the call straightaway, wanting to talk to his friend and tutor, who had taught him at the institute.

'Hello, John. How are you?'

'Fine. I just wondered – no, hoped – that you would be coming.'

'Yes, I'm looking forward to it.'

'Any news?'

'Well, no, not really. Nothing that I want to talk about on the phone at any rate,' Geoffrey replied. 'The powers that be want to destroy my addiction unit by cutting the budget in half.'

'I'm sorry about that. I know how much it means to you and how hard you've worked. What will you do?'

'I've met a rather interesting woman,' he said suddenly.

'Name?'

'Annabel. She's in London staying with her sister.'

John told him about his holiday in Provence and the interest he'd developed in van Gogh and 'mourning mother syndrome'. The effect that mourning had on the personality of the mother brought them to ideas, which centred on the child. Geoffrey knew that John had read and admired the work of Edward Emery, an analyst who had written a paper entitled the 'The Ghost of the Mother'. This paper examined the mourning of a mother for a young child and how it can adversely affect the personality of the mother

This avid discussion led into ideas relating to the seed of personality and the realization that there was no fairground freak or dislocated personality that had not lain, at some time, in the womb of a loving mother and that it is both our genetic make-up and our actions that reveal this personality, whether wonderful or otherwise. They concluded, eventually, that handling the human personality is akin to handling that which is both unknown and unpredictable.

****

When the conversation drew to an end his thoughts returned to Judith. This woman troubled him deeply. The idea of…night…filled his head. How, he wondered, could there suddenly be a Judith without beauty? Yet there was. He wished he could get her to voice her thoughts, her wishes, and her fears. But a curtain had fallen between them. He fell asleep that night with these mysterious thoughts on his mind.

Morning came and led into a deeper wondering. He wanted to explore what he knew to be a mystery. There was a fascination to discover what lay beneath the mask. John felt that there was some aspect of this darkness that was drawing him ever closer. Why had he failed to spot it when he was in France? He concluded that his powers of observation must be failing and put it down to his age. Yet, at the same time, he understood that holidays are not the same as real life and that they are, in essence, an escape from reality. He considered the possibility of some form of psychotic breakdown or even bipolar catastrophe. What horror had entered into this woman's mind? He could still see the terror in her face as he recalled the day he'd seen her at the bus stop.

Yes, he thought, *something, or someone, has poisoned Judith's soul, but what – or who – can it be?*

He picked up the phone once more and spoke to his friend and colleague.

'Did you feel this only when you saw her at the bus stop?'

'Yes, that's what's so odd. I didn't pick it up in France. She looked utterly transformed,' John replied, with a faraway look in his eye.

As if a metamorphosis had occurred? Is that what you mean?'

'Exactly. That is exactly what I mean,' he said slowly.

'I see.'

'She looked so…lonely, you see,' he replied, vaguely aware of a tear running down his cheek.

'Well, of course, it may be that something has happened to her. Do you think?'

'She's met her own terror.'

After hanging up the phone he took off his glasses made tea and toast, and just as he was contemplating the virtues of strawberry – as opposed to damson – jam, the phone went. It was Geoffrey again. John breathed a sigh of relief when he heard his voice.

He'd rung, he said, because of the anxiety that surrounded a particular client and his wife. There was, he acknowledged, a terror that she endured and that she lived with on an almost daily basis. Her husband was the most violent alcoholic he'd ever met. He acknowledged his feelings of helplessness in trying to support his wife and family in these dark, terrible times. John asked how long he'd been his patient.

'Oh, for years, must be seven, at least. He's been coming in and out for a long time. The longest he's been sober is three weeks. I've tried so many different things but all to no avail. He's engaged in group therapy, art therapy, psychotherapy – the lot!' Geoffrey exclaimed.

'For one so young, you have shown great patience. But then, I always knew you to be an exceptional student.'

'Do you believe yourself to be a physician of the soul, as Jung thought himself?'

'If I'm not a true Jungian, then I'm not anything. It's taken a whole lifetime to reach the point I'm at. It takes a long, long time; even now, I flounder. There are people, clients, who phase me. I can't see any way through. This woman is like that. She's not a client of mine. She's a friend of a friend. You see, it was pouring with rain, and she had no shoes on and no mac, so instinctively, I leapt off the bus and went over to her. I couldn't comprehend... She was altered in almost every particular. I couldn't grasp it. She seemed almost...possessed.'

'It's alchemy; something occurs, allowing an alteration to the inner, psychic landscape. You know how it is. I've seen it myself. But in my experience, it always follows an event or an action.'

'Lady Macbeth had her mind in her hand,' John said suddenly.

'Why on earth did you say that?'

'I've no idea. No idea at all.'

'You think the same could be said of Judith? She, too, had her mind in her hand?'

'It must have occurred to me as a possibility, or I wouldn't have mentioned it.'

'No, indeed, you wouldn't,' Geoffrey said slowly, realizing how troubled his friend was.

'We are not beasts of the field. We care deeply for one another,' he replied.

John quickly brought the conversation to a close and decided to go for a walk in Kensington Gardens to clear his head. It didn't help. He concluded, while gazing at the ducks on the round pond, that Judith was essentially a bloody, yet primitive organism.

He spent most of the night awake. He tossed and turned during his hopeless search for sleep. He thought of Claude and how happy and carefree he'd seemed in Provence, and how in love both his friend and Judith had been.

****

The next time he spoke to Geoffrey, John asked him about the woman he'd met and learnt that she had been sent to Handford by the Department of Health to advise on ways to end the deficit or, at least, reduce it, which – Geoffrey said – she was determined to do, no matter what. John enquired a little about her background, and gradually the penny dropped. He couldn't believe what he was hearing. He knew this woman. She'd lived with Claude. It was Annabel, he was sure, but to make certain, he asked Geoffrey how long she'd been in post at Handford.

'Oh, not long, not long at all. It must have been May because that was when I returned from India, and she was there then. A deficit discussion with her was my first task after returning from holiday.'

John thought back to Provence. Claude had told him clearly that Annabel had decided to take a job in Handford.

It has to be the same Annabel – a strange mixture of the clever, the kindly. He decided that the best thing he could do was to say nothing. He felt uneasy, troubled, and very anxious.

John spent most of that night awake, tossing and turning, which was unusual for him. He found Judith to be constantly on his mind. Eventually, he determined to ring Claude the next morning and to keep ringing until he answered.

The night was endless, or so it seemed. When he did sleep, he dreamt about stormy seas and a boat that he saw sinking. He tried to save the crew, but as he tried to drag them out of the sea, they turned into large fish.

When he woke up he recalled the night that had passed and the vivid dream he'd had. What was it saying to him? It was warning him of danger, the danger of trying to save people from themselves. The sea, in the dreamworld represents emotion. He went on to think about personal destiny and whether we are masters of our own destiny when so much evidence is to the contrary. He looked out of his bedroom window as the sun shot thick streaks of crimson across the sky, turning it blood red. As he gazed at it he felt more determined than ever to phone Claude and find out how Judith was. He counted the hours, even the minutes, until that became a possibility.

At 8 a.m. – with his heart pounding in his chest – he picked up the phone.

'Hello, hello it's John.'

'I've not heard from you for ages,' Claude replied with reproach in his voice.

'I've been very busy.'

'I wish you'd come to see me.'

'Are you all right?'

'No. One of my colleagues has had a heart attack, so I've had to fill in. It's keeping me together for the time being. I'm burying myself in my work.'

'Why do you want me to come and see you if you're so busy? Is something wrong?'

'Pretty much everything. Judith's mother died at the end of July. I don't know who she is any more. I want you to put her together again…to find the person who she was in Provence, the one who mixed one hundred and one shades of green. I…I don't know what to do.'

John had not expected this; he detected the note of horror in Claude's voice. 'I see.'

John sat with his head in his hands. He knew that he shouldn't have been so abrupt, dismissive even; he was upset. He didn't want Claude to know.

He set out on a long walk across London. He entered into that silent meditation that was common for him at times like these. The silence took him into himself. He allowed visions to pass unhindered through his mind and out towards the ocean.

****

Annabel wondered how Claude was and what was going on in his life. She realized that a large part of her missed London and the sheer exuberance of the great city. She missed rush hour and the mass of people with different faces. She even missed shouting at them when they trod on her feet on the Tube. On the surface, all seemed to be going well for her in Handford. She thrived on the antagonism at the hospital. She felt steel in her veins where she knew blood should be, but there were moments when she felt lonely.

She picked up her mobile phone to confirm the time of her arrival at her sister's flat. She was longing for the next day to dawn so she could drive away from Handford and back to London.

'I can't wait to see you. It seems as if you've been there forever,' Ruth replied.

'I miss Westbourne Grove, you, London – everything.'

'We'll do all the things we usually do – lots of retail therapy, lots of talking.'

'Lots of eating, but most of all, laughing. That's what I've missed most.' 'What about that man you met? You know, what's his name?'

'Geoffrey. Well, there's a whole evening's conversation just waiting to happen. But it's not what you want to hear, so be warned.'

Chapter Eight

Sam went to see his daughter. It was a dark dismal October day, and he'd not been for some time. When he came in, Judith retreated to the bedroom. She didn't want to see anyone, and yet she watched closely through the window as he walked to his car and got in. She observed his height and the determined gait that had always made her feel safe. She felt sad as he drove away. She imagined the rain pouring down the windscreen like liquid metal; she feared it might obliterate his vision. Dark clouds covered the whole sky with a thick grey haze.

How long this night will be, she thought. How lovely it would have been to have his company. This was impossible now, and she could imagine no time when it would be otherwise.

After he left, she got out a black silk scarf and wrapped it around her head so that her hair was covered. Alabaster foundation covered her face. It was exactly as she wished; she was simply a canvas. Loose porcelain powder completed the look.

In her wardrobe, she found a long black velvet dress that she'd bought at Portobello market. She stepped into it, recalling that Wagner always stroked velvet when he composed. Snippets of his music filled her head, leading to those childhood memories. She recalled the times her mother played on the piano; it matched so well her self-absorption. Once again, Judith's internal apothecary produced visual images of the police arriving and taking her mother away in a van. She had wondered where were they taking her. She hadn't seen her again for a long, long time. Sometimes she'd thought her mother was dead, but her father had said she wasn't, and for some reason, she had believed him. She'd always believed him. The trust had been implicit. It still was, and that was what made this separation so hard to bear.

Black gloves covered her hands, and dark leather shoes her feet. She looked in the mirror and saw a study in black. She was about to venture out when she saw her father returning for no apparent reason that she could understand. But, then, she understood nothing at this time.

Silently, they walked together arm in arm. Memories hurtled across her mind like meteorites across a blackened sky. She recalled the day she'd arrived at the house, the smell of vomit, and then there was a vacancy – perhaps a vacancy of mind, perhaps a vacancy of personality – as if she herself had vanished. The raindrops ran down her leather gloves. She noticed the patterns they made, the tiny grooves in the leather. She turned away from her father and returned to her flat amid memories that imprisoned her and led her home.

When she arrived, it was 5 p.m. exactly. She put the bread into the toaster and placed the pots of jam in front of her. There was a choice of strawberry, raspberry, loganberry, and damson. After staring at them for a few seconds, she thought, *Which do I want?* She dipped her slender finger into the raspberry and appreciated the thick softness, the intense shade of red, and the taste that transported her to hot summer days. Then she dipped her finger into the strawberry and licked the pink nectar as lumps of fruit exploded on her tongue, evoking memories of Wimbledon finals day. The loganberry, she decided at once, was too sour. Damson was king of the sweet and the sour and was the colour of venous blood. She consumed the whole loaf of bread and the entire jar of damson jam. As she ate, she observed the torrential rain pouring down the windowpane.

She wanted to wash, to wash herself away, so she ran a hot bath and immersed herself in the water. She thought of total immersion.

Eventually, she got out and wrapped herself in a towel. Slowly and fearfully, she climbed into bed. The sky didn't open, as she thought it should, and let her through. No, it was a bird that sat on her bed.

There was shouting in her nightmares, shouting that turned to wailing and then the cawing of vultures as they circled before landing on the corpse. When she woke up, she found the white sheets soaking wet. She entered her studio, where the dream transformed itself into something more concrete, more real, and certainly more tangible. She painted. And as she did so, images fled across her mind. At one point, it was her mother who held the paintbrush. She gave it into her keeping, and the style and depth of the painting changed. She recognized as if in her mother's hand, the creative energy deepened and charged itself as if from within. There were no limits now, as Judith's physicality disappeared and merged with her dead mother's, so that the limits of her own body and her own ability were no more. She was merely a cypher through which colour and form travelled.

When the clouds covered the earth in a thick dark blanket, Sam knocked on the door. Judith looked out nervously.

'Why don't you go away?' she said.

'I don't want to.'

'I don't want to see you.'

'Who do you want to see?'

'No one.'

'Judith, let me in. Just for a few minutes. Please.'

She opened the door. He went inside. There was chaos. He picked up the card that Claude had left and read what it said: "John Antony, PhD, Jungian psychotherapist/psychoanalyst." There was an address in Moscow Road, followed by a phone number and a tiny email address at the bottom.

She watched intently as Sam turned the card over in his hand. Then he turned it back again and read the address. It was, she knew, only round the corner from where he lived, near where she'd killed his wife. She wanted him to contact John, being unable to do so herself. There was a paralysis of action, emanating from her belief that she was now untouchable. No human being would want contact. There was loneliness. She observed her father for several minutes before retreating. He quietly opened the door into the studio before he left. There she sat painting, her hand trembling as she drew the paintbrush along the canvas.

The portrait made her feel uncomfortable. On the canvas, two creatures appeared together, a bird and a woman. The lines were strong and certain along the jawline but softer and diffuse in the eye socket where the bird's nest was. The skull was filled with birds' feathers of contrasting colours. Tears filled her father's eyes. They ran down his face. He stroked the edge of the business card and read the email address over and over again, jant5@ btinternet.com, and determined at that moment to contact John Antony. Impulsively, without invitation, he hugged his daughter.

He left and walked home in the freezing cold and rain.

After he'd gone, Judith came to realize that, without warning, he'd found himself a widower. Yet she was no longer linked to him. The bond they'd had for all these years was broken. In effect, they were strangers. The truth, as far as she was concerned, was that he'd been either too busy or too ignorant to understand what had been going on in her head. He'd buried himself in work and had made a lot of money buying and selling property. She hoped that, before the truth came out, he'd help somehow, anyhow.

CHAPTER NINE

Sam turned into Pembridge Square, marched up the steps of his home, placed the key in the lock, and turned it. Once inside, he closed the door and looked around. Virginia's clothes were still in the hall. He wanted them out of the way. He went to the attic and found boxes and bags, hurled them down the stairs, and stuffed all her hats and bags into the boxes. He went into the bedroom that they'd shared and rummaged through her chest of drawers, pulling out nightdresses, blouses, bras, and knickers. He stuffed them into plastic bags. Underneath the bed, he discovered thirteen gin bottles, which he tossed downstairs one after the other. The bottles crashed against one another as they fell. Once in the hall, Sam shoved them into cardboard boxes before opening the front door and throwing them into the bins, listening to the smashing, crashing sound they made. In the lounge, he pulled her paintings off the walls and tore the curtains down. She had to be eradicated from his life, as though she'd never lived.

The following morning, he loaded up his jeep and took the whole lot to Oxfam in Westbourne Grove. Once he'd unloaded, the shop was filled to bursting point with Virginia's belongings. He told the girl in the shop that he would return soon with more books and dresses.

He enjoyed his large espresso at Carluccio's. While drinking it he realized how hungry he was, so he looked at the menu and ordered a large plate of ravioli, filled with sundried tomatoes and freshly made pesto, and a green salad drenched in olive oil. He couldn't decide whether it tasted so good because he was so hungry or whether it was, in fact, the most delicious meal he'd ever had.

He was famished, and as he ate, thoughts of his daughter returned. He wondered, as only a father can wonder, what her future might be and what he could do to help. He wanted so much to understand all that had gone on and all that would come after. This mystery held him in its spell every hour of every day. He finished his meal, got out his mobile phone, and tapped John Antony's number into it from the card he had in his pocket.

There was no answer; desperation grabbed his heart and held it tight. A lone tear coursed down his face. He didn't have the energy to to wipe it away, and soon another followed and another, until eventually a stream of saltwater was flowing down his cheeks.

A woman from a nearby table glanced in his direction. He heard her say to her friend, 'No, you're right, I know you are. I can't possibly go back to all that.'

She smiled at him as he left the restaurant, a generous smile. He appreciated it on that cold, dark afternoon and realized then that there was nothing he needed more than the smile of a perfect stranger.

On returning to his house, he went upstairs for another load of clothes. The dresses were more difficult; they held her perfume on them. The scent hit him as he opened her wardrobe. It sent him reeling as the memories of their life together fell across his mind—the moment when he took her hand and kissed it after the birth of Harry, the moment eighteen months later when little Harry died. Memories are like the drawers of an apothecary; they are small and most of the time they are closed, but when you open them, you may find healing balm or you may discover poison.

Virginia's scent had the capacity to send him into mysterious worlds; images sat with him. The cupboards held soft velvet dresses that he loved. He touched them, knowing them to be exquisite works of art embroidered with fine silk. When she had worn them, he'd felt the kind of pride that only a man can know when walking hand in hand with a woman. He ripped them to pieces one by one, watching as the strips of coloured velvet fell around him, covering the floor like a huge mosaic. The colours embedded themselves within him like a meditation. He slept there on the floor among the perfumed velvet and dreamt that the strips of fabric were hanging on the walls like tapestries. The following morning, found him sleeping until 11 a.m.

Immediately on waking, he phoned John Antony.

'Hello?'

'Hello, hello. You don't know me. My name is Samuel Bach.'

'I see. Can I help you in some way? It's John Antony speaking. I always forget to say that when I answer the phone. Very remiss of me, I know, but there it is.'

Sam warmed to this individual who had a voice like honey.

'I wonder if I could make an appointment to see you. A friend of mine left your card. He seemed to think you might be able to give advice on a private matter.'

'I see. May I ask who gave you my card?' John replied. 'His name is Claude.'

'Ah, yes. His father and I were great friends. When would you like to come along?'

'Are you free today, by any chance? The matter is rather urgent. The card says you're a Jungian psychoanalyst and that you have a PhD. Is that correct?'

'Yes, that's right,' John replied. 'I was a professor at the Jungian Institute before I retired. Well, let me see. My diary, where on earth is it? Oh yes, I was sitting on it. This afternoon, you said. I could make 4 p.m. I like to make the first meeting quite relaxed.'

'How much do you charge?'

'Nothing for the first session. I find out if I can be of any assistance, we discuss your needs, your problems, so to speak, and then we go from there. Do you see?'

'Thank you. I have your address on my card. I'll arrive at four this afternoon.'

Sam put the phone down and made himself some toast and honey. It tasted good. He made himself several slices. When he'd finished, he got an old wooden chair he'd bought down Portobello and pushed it up to the bookshelves. All Virginia's books were here, from Zadie Smith to Iris Murdoch. He opened one or two before hurling them to the floor, he placed them in boxes and put them in the car, loading them one by one, reading a few phrases here and there. He found a shelf full of Ian McEwan's novels and discovered that she had purchased his latest, *Solar*, which he'd found amusing – yet they'd never discussed it. He remembered a conversation they'd had about *Atonement*, which she had thought futile; what was done was done, and it could never be undone, no matter what you did. She seemed to have little concept of remorse, regret, or sadness. He remembered disagreeing, saying that the least one could do was to attempt to limit the damage and to try to make amends. The night had ended with hostility and tension, with Virginia saying that he constantly denigrated her and her opinions. The following day, she was drunk, and the poison held her in its grasp once more. He'd escaped – gone to work and worked incessantly for weeks on end. He worked. That was how it was. She drank: He worked.

He put these memories out of his mind and piled up more and more books, placing them in the car before taking them down to the Oxfam shop, where there was a very young girl but not the same one as the day before. She was more accommodating and kinder.

After he'd unloaded the books, Sam went once more to Carluccio's for coffee because it was, quite simply, the best coffee in London. He sat there wondering what the afternoon meeting with John Antony would be like. He felt apprehensive about it, yet, at the same time, he knew that he had to do something, and this was the only thing he could think of. He ate a large plate of sardines, which were delicious; paid the bill; and left rapidly. He drove back to his house. It looked empty and forlorn yet spacious. Impatiently, he wiped away the tears that streamed down his face as he left the house.

Very, very slowly he walked to see John Antony. He entered the Greek Orthodox Church at the top of Moscow Road. He opened the massive door and thought the walls looked as though they had been dipped in solid gold. The sun fell through the stained-glass window, causing his body to shudder as his eyes drank in the beauty. He sat in the pew, allowing the atmosphere of this holy place to invade his being, to pour its molten liquid into the innermost reaches of his body; his mind; and, eventually, his soul.

The street was empty when he emerged. On arrival at John Antony's house, he rang the bell. The door opened, and in he went. Sam loved the place as soon as he got there. He looked at the books on all the bookshelves; they stretched as far as the eye could see. There was a strong smell of beeswax, and an oak table sat in the middle of the room beside an ancient leather chair with horsehair sticking out of it. There were two more chairs of indeterminate age. He felt immediately at home. In a far corner, he spied a computer that was covered up with a large lace tablecloth, and rather a beautiful tablecloth at that. He smiled to himself.

'Good afternoon. I'm John Antony.'

Sam thought his was, above all, a kindly face and realized that this was what he wanted more than anything. What he craved was, quite simply, the milk of human kindness.

'I'm Sam Bach,' he replied.

'What an illustrious name. How fortunate you are. Please, sit down while I fetch the tea.'

Sam examined the books from his armchair, knowing full well that a man can be judged by the books in his library. He could see *The Complete Works of C. G. Jung* as well as books on ancient alchemical texts. There was also The Interpretation of Dreams by Freud and every major religious work. On the third shelf, on the left-hand side, he spied a huge collection of William Blake's works, next to which sat *The Complete Works of William Shakespeare.*

John returned, carrying a large teapot, a couple of cups, and some buns on a tray. Sam grasped hold of the cup of tea that was being offered to him.

'Now, tell me. How I can help you?' John said, after settling himself in his armchair.

'My daughter's not well. I mean, she's not...'

'The same?' John interposed.

'No... I don't know what to do. I...just don't know what to do.'

'Do you want to name her, or do you prefer to call her your daughter?' 'Well, she is my daughter.'

'Is she anything else?' John asked.

'She's a painter, an artist.'

'I see. Do you want help for yourself or for your daughter?'

'My daughter, it's since her mother died, you see.'

'You still haven't given her a name,' said John.

'Her name is Judith,' Sam murmured, noticing immediately the look of amazement, almost disbelief, on the other man's face. 'Do you know her, by any chance?'

John ignored the question. Sam's confusion spilled out into the room and tainted the atmosphere. Eventually, John admitted he'd met her in France while on holiday. A protracted silence followed.

Sam wondered if he should leave but was reluctant to do so. He'd taken a liking to this man and didn't know where else to turn. 'Does that make any difference?' he asked.

'It should do. Strictly speaking, it means that I can't charge money. It would be unprofessional, but then, I am retired.'

'Why would you do it then, if not for money?'

'What, I wonder, can I do for you?' Sam asked.

Sam felt somewhat taken aback by this response, but as he reflected upon it, he came to realize the wisdom of it. 'I'm not accustomed to charity.'

'I don't see charity in that way. We all need help sometimes in our lives.'

'What, I wonder, can I do for you?' Sam asked.

'Book tokens are always welcome. You can never have too many books,' he said, smiling.

'You can have them – in abundance.'

Sam thought about the beautiful creature that was his daughter, and wondered if this man would really be able to help her. It was possible that this kindly soul held in his hands the seeds of recovery; this impression mingled, tangled, and jangled around in his head like a tin can bashing down the wall of despair. There was some magnetism in in the character in front of him.

This, he thought, is the person…who can connect us together again. This, more than anything, was what he wanted.

'We met on holiday in France. We conversed a good deal,' the old man mused.

'I see, I see. Would that be the Vincent van Gogh holiday she's just returned from?'

'Well, it's several months ago, back in the spring. But yes, that's the one.' 'You wouldn't know her if you could see her now. She's almost unrecognizable,' he replied.

Sam looked at this man and wondered, once more, what he could do. In his mind's eye there was a metaphysical connection already. He grasped at this straw as drowning men do.

'Would you like to come and see me yourself, instead?' John asked suddenly.

'It's since her mother's death that this all came about. Something's happened.'

'You are grieving yourself.'

'I'm out of my depth. That's why I've come to you.'

'I understand. How old were you when Judith was born?'

'My wife and I were both twenty-three. Judith's gone. I want my daughter back. I don't know where she's gone.'

'I will do my best to return your daughter, if that's what she wants, Mr Bach, but – and it's a big but – she must agree. You can only help someone if, at some level at least, they want to be helped.'

'Thank you so much. You can never know how grateful I am for this. Maybe there is some favour I can do for you – now or at some future time.'

'Goodbye.'

****

The two men parted and Sam walked slowly home. He stopped off again at the Greek Orthodox Church and gazed once more at the icons. He couldn't remember the last time he'd prayed, but he knelt down, placing his head in his hands. A strange sense came to him, a feeling that the icons were moving, that the stillness was disturbed, that there was a spirit, or at least a presence, that was not mortal and had no bodily form. Images of a bloody crucifixion, of sharp thorns embedded in his skull filled his mind. His mind travelled into another dimension. His world was changed. It would never be quite the same again. The day he'd found his wife dead had been a day of transfiguration. While he sat in the church, the realization dawned on him that something lay hidden, something dark that he did not know. There was a secret that had yet to be told. In the presence of these icons, something was revealed. They gave him an insight. He felt certain – as he sat there in that church, on that day – that Judith's love for her mother was not of such magnitude that her death could have caused this demonic alteration. It was the first time he had allowed the word demonic to attach itself to his daughter, but that was what it was; it was as if she were possessed. Rage emerged in that church, but there was also truth. He left and walked rapidly to Judith's flat.

She was surprised to see him. She opened the door. He placed his hands on her cheekbones and brought his face next to hers.

'The truth. Tell me the truth. I'm not leaving until you tell me the truth. I want to know. What happened? I've got a right to know.'

'You have no right to know anything. You left me.'

'What happened? Judith, tell me what happened,' he pleaded.

'You left me, you went and left me…'

'What happened to you? Did something happen to you the day she died?'

Judith ran to the kitchen. He followed and saw something in her eyes, something he'd never seen before, except in productions of Macbeth. How can this something have grown? Where can it have come from, this look? Where did it germinate? Where had it been born? His mind flashed back to his days at drama school when a tutor had said, 'It's in your eyes. Tell the story with your eyes. Let them see it in your eyes.' He realized she was telling the story with her eyes, and what she was telling, he couldn't bear to see. The shock of it drove him away. He wanted to be as far away from her as he could get.

He left immediately. The night air was cold. He couldn't wait to get home. What he wanted was solitude. He wanted to slip between the sheets and feel the familiarity of his bed. As he slept, he dreamt of Judith. He was with her in a large building, possibly a hospital, and as he sat there, her eyelids quivered and turned yellow. Her pupils turned to ochre, the whites of her eyes to a mustard colour. Her face resembled a map with blue threaded veins running across it. A doctor, a priest, and an alchemist appeared, carrying a pot with hawthorn leaves and rowan berries floating in it. The three stirred the mixture. The priest poured in thick honey. The doctor added locusts that had lost their wings. The alchemist added birds' feathers and black blood. The mixture was applied to Judith's eyes. They vanished; empty sockets emerged. They applied the concoction to her body; black feathers appeared. There were no wings.

The dream faded. Sam woke up to find that it was late morning. He lay there thinking about the events of the night and about his daughter. He considered what she had said to him, and he knew all of it was true.

'How could I be so hideous? It's me who should be going to see John Antony and not Judith.' There were, he knew, things he could have done to change the situation, yet he had done nothing. He had allowed it to go on for years and years. It was, he concluded, a kind of paralysis. Did I not care? he asked himself. How could I not care? He plunged headlong into self-examination; guilt and self-loathing filled every crevice of his being.

The phone rang. It was Claude. 'Judith phoned me at midnight,' he said. 'She sounded…broken, if that's the right word to use. I went over there, and she just sat crying, saying you'd been there.'

'It's true. I had been there. It was difficult, very difficult. It's as if she's in some poisonous dialogue with herself – with everyone and everything. I've been to see John Antony, as you suggested. Hopefully, he'll help. He seemed kind and-'

'Thank God for that. He'll do all he can. We never know how much we love our mothers until they're dead. I know I didn't. Maybe…'

It has more to do with hate than love, I fear, Sam thought to himself. There was silence. Neither party knew what to say to the other. Sam put down the phone and worked meticulously, dismantling Virginia's study – the books, her DVDs (of which there were thousands) and the notes she'd made while studying at the London School of Fashion. He glanced at them and wasn't surprised that she'd left with a distinction in her final exams. If she hadn't been pregnant with Harry when she was just twenty… if only,' if only…none of this would have happened…

But, he concluded, *it did happen*. Virginia was pregnant with Harry, and Harry had died.

This routine, this ritual of disposing of her possessions – taking them down to the Oxfam shop and then having lunch at Carluccio's – became his daily activity. Particular garments triggered certain memories. One day, it was a pair of Chanel pyjamas in pure white silk with black edging. He remembered buying them for her birthday, and how delighted she had been to receive them. His mind brought her memory to life as vividly as if it were yesterday. Oh, the joy of it! For a moment, these perfect garments had taken it upon themselves to lighten his load. He put them to his face. He could smell their creaminess and felt the caress that is silk. She had kept the beautiful Chanel bag that they came in. Slowly, with infinite tenderness, he placed them in his briefcase. As he did so, he sensed a gentle healing. A balm coursed through his veins, causing tears to fall once more. He wiped them away, placed the boxes in the car, and set off for Westbourne Grove.

The lady in the Oxfam shop that morning was both beautiful and elderly. She was dressed in a long beige skirt. Her face was that of a woman who had lived an interesting life, and in some way, she reminded him of his own mother. Together they unloaded the boxes. She said how grateful Oxfam was for his exceptional donations and assured him that the money was to be targeted specifically for the starving in the developing world.

'Thank you so much,' she said.

Without replying, he opened his briefcase and handed her the packet that contained the Chanel pyjamas.

'No,' she murmured. 'Take them away with you. This is neither the time nor the place to part with them.'

Sam looked at her and knew that this was exactly what his own mother would have said. 'What's your name?' Sam asked.

'Heather,' she replied.

'My mother's name,' he said. 'That was my mother's name.'

'Lucky mother,' she replied.

Carluccio's was empty that morning, which disappointed him. He needed people's chatter. What he wanted was life and, he decided, a plate of ravioli filled with ricotta cheese and drenched with thick tomato sauce.

It was around 2 p.m. when two young women walked in. They sat at a table near him and ordered large cappuccinos. He saw at once that one was crying. She was the lady who had smiled such a generous smile the day before.

'You always think you're right about everything,' said the lady who was crying.

'Well, what do you want me to say? What do you want me to do?' 'Nothing.'

Sam's ravioli duly arrived. He was hungry. He'd had no breakfast and, he dimly remembered, no supper. A large bowl of salad stood next to the ravioli, with a bottle of Chianti. He heard one of the women at the table next to him say that she thought his meal looked divine. She was right. It was divine; as he ate, his mood changed and, thus, his state of mind. He immersed himself in the flavours, and all of them brought Italy to mind. Virginia had loved Italy, Tuscany in particular because of the colour and the peachy softness of the land. It was their land, the place they'd holidayed and probably where Harry had been conceived. He'd thought at one time, when Judith was about five, of buying a property there, where they could live – a place where they could escape from the drunken tyranny that was Virginia. But nothing had come of it. He wasn't quite sure why, but he recognized that it had been a mistake; that is what he should have done.

Why didn't I do that? he asked himself.

The two women on the next table chattered away, their closeness apparent. He heard the name 'Claude' and focused his attention on their conversation.

'You can't. It's impossible. You've carved out a new life for yourself in Handford, and you've been so happy the last few months. Go on, admit it.'

'I admit it,' said the crying woman.

'You told me you'd found this man…'

'It's his house – babies would be so happy there, under the apple trees in the orchard. And then there's Carl, the dog. He's so lovely too.'

'But you haven't any babies.'

'No, but I could have. If only I could love Geoffrey, but I don't. I wish I did. If only…I did.'

'I don't understand you. I really don't. Shall we have some cake? You might stop crying. I think you're exhausted.'

'Oh yes, let's have cake. I like the espresso one. I think it's called torte.'

'Yes, it's lovely. I'll get some.'

She went to the counter. The queue was quite long, and this enabled Sam to get a closer look at the lady who was crying. He wondered what she was so sad about. Her face, he observed, was almond-shaped, her hair was the colour of fire and shone as if it had been polished. This woman was not beautiful, by any standards, but she was certainly alluring. This intrigued Sam. He wanted to find out more. His curiosity had been aroused. It was a diversion from a troubled life.

The cake duly arrived and more coffee. Sam's eyes glanced at the lady who bought the cake. She looked very anxious and rather perturbed.

'It's no good being annoyed or cross or whatever you are.'

The other lady placed the cake on the table with two forks before she spoke.

'I'm not cross. It's just so difficult, Annabel. You're clever. You sailed through university and came out with a first. I, on the other hand, became a hairdresser. Yet here we are again, having a similar conversation to the one we had nine months ago, when you made the brave decision to take the prestigious job in Handford and leave a whole heap of misery behind. I thought you'd succeeded. I'm disappointed in a way, just disappointed.'

'It's so lovely, the house. It's sixteenth century with a thatched roof, one of those black and white houses with lots of beams.'

'Do stop talking about the bloody house, the house is an irrelevance.' 'Oh, look! Here's Heather. I haven't seen her for ages.'

'Annabel, Ruth what a delightful surprise! And you're eating my favourite cake!' Heather exclaimed.

Heather turned round and saw Sam at the table nearby. 'Hello again.' Sam was pleased and, at the same time, mildly irritated, rather as a minor spy might feel if his cover had been blown. He muttered, 'Hello.' He was utterly engrossed in the conversation.

Heather went to the counter and got herself a large slice of espresso torte and a flat white coffee. She sat down next to Annabel and listened to the story as related by Ruth. At last, Annabel said, 'It has so much wildlife. Hedgehogs come and sip the milk. Geoffrey always puts it out for them.'

Sam was finding it difficult to maintain his equilibrium. He felt, at last, laughter spreading across his insides the kind of laughter he thought he'd never experience again.

Oh, God, he thought, *this is priceless!* He ordered an ice cream and an espresso, got a small book of poetry out of his pocket, and pretended to read while continuing to listen to the conversation.

'Do you love him, this man you met in Handford?' asked Heather. 'No, that's why I'm crying. I wish to God I did, but I don't,' Annabel replied with utter certainty.

'Such, my dear, is the nature of love.'

'I'm confused…'

'Confused about what exactly?' Heather replied. 'You don't seem very confused to me. This man in Hereford has a lovely house and a career, and would make a good father for your children, but you don't love him. So, wherein lies the confusion?'

'About, about…'

'About that damned Claude, I suppose!' exclaimed Ruth.

At this point in the conversation, Sam almost choked on his espresso.

It spilt all over his shirt. He ordered another, which, luckily, was slow to arrive.

'When I fell in love with Claude, he was a broken vessel,' replied Annabel.

Sam's feelings mellowed. He was finding it more and more difficult not to look at the face of this sad lady, but he maintained his self-discipline and kept his eyes focused on his small book of poetry.

'I don't understand, but you must stop this crying. I'm beginning to think this job in Handford is too much of a strain. You are behaving most oddly,' said Ruth, sternly.

'I can't bear the thought of going back to Handford. I can't even bear the thought of Geoffrey.'

Sam realized that this was drawing him, at least temporarily, away from his own particular misery and into somebody else's. Suddenly, Annabel's eyes rested on his face, and a sweetness filled him as he caught the wheel of the autumn sunshine in one of her ears. He thought she seemed wounded, her body merely the platform from which the wound hung, as if in mid-air.

'You have to go back to Handford, and that's the end of the matter. You have a contract there. It'll all sort itself out once you start work. As soon as you stop, you get like this. I've seen it before,' Ruth replied.

'I have a strong feeling that I'm supposed to be here, in London. I don't know why.'

'It may be your inner voice. It's always wise to heed it,' said Heather. She got up, gave Annabel and Ruth a kiss on the cheek, and left.

'I have to go too. I just can't take any more of this crying and this nonsense, because that's what it is – nonsense,' Ruth said, 'I'll see you at home later.'

The restaurant door closed behind them, shutting out the October chill. Sam watched the crying lady closely as waves of gentleness washed over him. He wondered how he could help. She got up, smiled at him, and wandered out into the street. He followed her and asked if she was all right. She nodded and smiled once more. Sam felt a stab of recognition as she went but was mystified as to its origin, not realizing that what he wished for, more than anything, was to be able to access his feelings, to be able to howl. He needed to liberate his own grief, to cry as she had done. He was, however, a man, and such outpourings of emotion were rare, if not impossible. Initially, at the very beginning, his empathy for Annabel had originated within his own despair. He realized that his own existence was corrosive at this moment in time. It was grief his sense of self-preservation prevented access to his inner darkness. He wanted to rid himself of it.

He knew the feeling was directly connected with Judith. A part of him wanted to wash her away, this daughter whom he'd loved all his life. He was disintegrating. He felt a loosening, an ache in the centre of his stomach that never went away. He had to break into something, or someone, in order to save himself.

He turned and gave Annabel a long lingering look. His shoulders softened. His lower lip trembled slightly. The terrible pain he'd endured the night before subsided. The air around him bustled and hummed; there was so much life there in the world, so much life within. This awareness spread slowly around him as he looked at the crying lady in the distance.

He knew he had an endless supply of stuff belonging to his wife that he could take to Oxfam. He wanted to take all her clothes to Oxfam, there was a famine in Ethiopia, and at least he was doing something.

He wanted to learn more; he had to learn more. His curiosity had been piqued about the sad, somewhat attractive woman. He wished that he could cry as she could, go to bed and howl about his wife and his child. He couldn't even get drunk because then his judgement would be clouded, and he knew better than most where that would lead.

No, he thought, a bottle of Chianti at lunchtime will soften the world a little and remind me of the Tuscan sun, and that's exactly what I need right now.

Who, he wondered, was the crying lady?

CHAPTER TEN

Judith was, however, a very different animal. Her coping mechanisms were strained to the limit. She paid her first visit to John Antony. It was strained, and little was said. It was in silence that they sat in his study, surrounded on all sides by the books that he'd amassed in the course of a lifetime. The hour passed, without comment. She got up and, asking if she could come and visit him at some future time, left.

She walked home through darkened streets and cold rain. She watched as the water ran down the drains and thought this was her rightful place, down there with the water rats, not walking on pavements with human beings, for she had destroyed the very thing that made her human. She no longer belonged to any species. It was a slow, dismal journey, and she found it long and tiresome. She was so often tired and in need of comfort, but comfort never came. There was this position of existence; as long as her heartbeat continued, then existence was inevitable.

When she arrived home, she went into the study and painted until midnight. The canvas came to life and was, in essence, her life now. It was only through the medium of paint that she could emerge, even for short periods of time, from the guilt and self-loathing that held her in its grasp. This had no link with repentance; it was not remorse she felt but absence, absence of everything. It was as if the landscape that is life – with all the highs and lows and all the colours of the rainbow – had been replaced by grey. This interminable landscape was the sea in which she lived. There was no sense of journeying to some other shoreline; this sea was becalmed and full of monsters that arose from deep water, emerging from beneath the skyline. They were real. She assumed her mother had awakened them from their slumbers when she died, when her life ended. This dead woman, who had dominion over them due to the nature of her death, controlled these creatures. Dark creatures did her bidding.

When she painted, they rested, but they wanted their own image portrayed. They were both vain and greedy.

She daren't leave them for long, or they would extract a terrible revenge and enter her consciousness in the hours of darkness. Whether she slept or not, they were there. She'd go to her room, cover herself with a duvet, and scream at the horrors around her as they alighted on her bed. Huge bats flew at her face, landing on her hair. Vultures flew around the space. She believed the death of her mother had prompted their arrival. She was, through her act, connected to murderers both past and present. She belonged to that group of individuals who had deprived another human being of life. She lay there and thought of others like herself and the acts they had perpetrated, the lives they had laid waste. The wasteland that followed this most heinous of crimes was her land now, and she inhabited it alone.

It was at this time that she realized that, unless she shared her crime with someone, life would be impossible; she could not live the rest of her life alone with this knowledge. She decided there and then to tell John Antony or, perhaps, her father. At least she knew that her father would never inform the police, but then, there was the question of forgiveness. Would he ever forgive her? This was the question.

Something within her was rising up, and it gave her no peace. She didn't know what to do or how to hold on. It was something within her heart that refused to die away. It burned there, this searing anguish. No matter how hard she tried, Judith could not get a grip on herself. Something was rising up within her, without ceasing. It caused her pain and would not quiet down. Crime lay heavily upon her soul. The house in which she lived became, at this time, a tomb from which she rarely, if ever, emerged. She lived alone with her demonic self. The ancient mystery of good and evil played itself out in Judith's head, the thought processes doing battle with one another and producing visions of hell and purgatory.

It was at this time that Judith succumbed to a dream in which all the world fell victim to the plague, and people's bodies were invaded by microscopic creatures that contained spirits who had will and great intelligence. People who were infested with these creatures became infected with them, as with a fever. All became infected with a terrible anxiety that they would infect someone else. They walked about beating their breasts, howling and wringing their hands. People killed one another for no apparent reason, and everyone tried to find a solution to the problem, but one could not be found. Fires broke out for no apparent reason. Famines occurred. Everyone perished.

When Judith awoke from this dream, she knew that she had been infected by the crime she had committed. She wondered what she was to do. Could she ever get better? What, if anything, could make her better? Could she ever be restored to her former self? The isolation into which she had descended was linked with this idea of infection, that someone might be affected by her presence. If they breathed the same air as her, would that be enough? Would it be the touch that would eventually seal their fate?

She found being alone had become tolerable only when she painted or slept. That was how she spent the hours of existence. She came to realize that, if evil existed, then good must also exist. It might, she reasoned, be possible to look for it too actively.

Chapter Eleven

Claude knocked on the door of John's flat. A stranger answered. It was a shock. It was unusual for the door to be opened by someone he didn't know.

'Is John in?'

'I believe he's in the bath, but he does seem to have been there for a long time. Do you know him well? Have you known him long?' the man asked.

All my life. He was a friend of my father's. What about you?'

'He was my tutor when I was at the Jungian Institute, so I've known him for ten years.'

At this opportune moment, John emerged from the bathroom dressed in a faded green dressing gown smelling of olive soap. Claude recalled the day they had gone to the local market in Provence and bought a year's supply of this gorgeous stuff. It was very cheap and came from an olive farm up in the hills, far away from civilization. The couple were kind and grateful that these two Englishmen should be so interested in their olive groves that they invited them to their farm, where they saw the old-fashioned press squeezing every drop of the aromatic green oil into waiting barrels. They took them into the little barn where they made the soap, the shampoo, the lotions and potions. He thought also of Judith's painting of the olive trees and how she'd always painted during those warm happy days in Provence. She'd held him with her beauty. A lone tear fell from his eyes. He wiped it away.

'Can I help, I wonder?' Geoffrey murmured.

'It's a memory, just a memory,' Claude replied. He found a glass and poured some wine into it.'Come and see Judith. She's gone crazy all of a sudden.'

'I've seen her already,' John murmured.

'What, since we've returned from France?'

'Yes.'

'Why didn't you tell me?'

'She asked me not to.'

'I see. When did you see her?'

'About three weeks ago. Her father wants me to see her professionally.' Claude didn't answer.

'I wish I could help you, but I work as a psychiatrist in Handford and I have to go home tomorrow,' Geoffrey said.

'Oh, I know someone who works in Handford at the hospital. She's a manager there. You might know her. John knows her.'

'Annabel's been a close friend of Claude's for the last six years.'

'She was very close to me when I was grieving.'

'She is very, very kind,' murmured John.

'I see,' Geoffrey replied, pouring himself another glass of wine. John made coffee and passed a cup to Claude, who took it with some reluctance. He'd never known it like this with John. It seemed as if he, too, had left him.

'Why didn't you tell me you'd seen her?'

'She asked me not to. In fact, she begged me not to.'

'Why? What on earth is going on?'

'I'm not exactly sure, and if I were, I couldn't tell you.'

'Her mother died...suddenly, or so it seems,' Claude said.

'Yes, I do know.'

Claude didn't admit it, even to himself, but he was afraid, very afraid – but he had no idea what of. The only way he could cope with the terror was by denying it. He decided then and there that he would bury himself in his work. God knew there was plenty of it. It seemed that John resented his questions, and even his presence, so he left and wended his way back home.

****

The following day, Geoffrey arrived back at Ferney House. Carl was delighted to see him. The garden was a mass of colour. Russet red and mustard yellow leaves hung from the trees. The orchard trees were heavy with ripe purple plums and variegated apples. Here was comfort and continuity, as well as the crop of next year's jam harvest. How well and contented he felt.

The messages on his answerphone were many, and he spent the next hour or so on the phone to his department. There had been an emergency connected to a patient of his who had a serious drink problem, which had been exacerbated during his absence. The family had come in asking for help and support. This concerned him, as it always did, so he went for a long cycle ride along the quiet lanes. It felt good exercising his leg muscles in the chilly evening air. He resented Annabel and the cuts she seemed determined to recommend to the trust. During the last few days, it had been constantly on his mind, and even the cycle ride could not distract him.

When he arrived back at Ferney House, it was getting dark. He sat down at his computer, but this only made matters worse, so he poured himself a whisky and wrote a long draft regarding the addiction unit and why he felt it to be of such vital importance to the people of Handford. It was 3 a.m. before he fell asleep. He woke up very suddenly the following morning, got dressed, and drove to the hospital in his car – a bright red Volkswagen Beetle convertible. He put an Amy Winehouse CD into the stereo and listened to this voice that he loved. A friend he'd trained with had treated her at the Priory. They both felt the same about her – she had a phenomenal talent, and it was tragic that no treatment regime, either in this country or in the States, could loosen the hold that addiction had on her mind and repair the damage it did to her body.

He thought about this as he drove to the county hospital. What was it, he wondered, this phenomena known as addiction? He believed it to be, first and foremost, a state of being – not a thing that you do but a thing that you are, like being old, being white, or being a child. This was a very controversial position. He knew that many within his own profession did not share it. He believed there existed a genetic predisposition to addiction, whether it be alcoholism, drug addiction, or food addiction, and then some stress factor triggered the gene, bringing the addiction to life. His method of treating addicts within his own unit was to look at the stress factor that caused the descending spiral of despair and, somehow, to change the dynamics within a given situation.

Support for the families of addicts he knew to be of primary importance. He worked tirelessly to prevent family disintegration, which was the most common result of addiction. The saddest part of his life was watching the children of addicts drawn inevitably into the web. The results were clear; the child will try to take care of and protect the addict from the world, from the consequences of their actions. The child then assumes the role of parent and takes on areas of responsibility that he or she has neither the mental nor emotional maturity to deal with. Geoffrey knew the damage to be enormous; often it could never be healed. But he and his team provided a support structure for the addict and their children so that the minors felt less isolated, less alone, and less frightened. He hoped they felt understood. So many in the hazy, dark world of addiction never feel that.

He retreated back into the world of work, returning to the job he loved, the people he knew, and the patients who needed him. *This is the world that matters*, he thought as he strode across the car park at the hospital. He arrived in the unit and had various meetings with members of staff during the day. He was brought up to date on all that was going on around him.

The next day, he had a review of the Reynolds family's case. He read through the notes and absorbed new information from social services saying that the son had been to school with a cut lip. Everything but work vanished from his mind.

CHAPTER TWELVE

Sam continued his daily routine of going to Oxfam with Virginia's clothes and having lunch and a bottle of Chianti at Carluccio's. He saw the woman who'd been crying a few days before. This time she was alone. She had a large cappuccino in front of her. Luckily the cafe was almost full, so he could legitimately ask whether he could share her table, to which she readily agreed.

'I saw you the other day,' she said.

'Yes.'

He could feel the pulse in his neck. Discomfort rose in his brain, digging its claws into that place behind his ear. A tiny joy had faded. He rooted around within himself, searching for it, trapped. At that moment, he realized how important it was that she should fall in love with him, right now, in this second – this very second. Does everything have to be analysed to the bone? Does there have to be an explanation? Can't something just happen?

How strong this is, he thought.

He was surprised at the vision that lay within and wondered how he could construct her from so little; a braid of veins, delicate with twists and bumps. He became focused, as if he had been told a secret. He looked at her; a sweetness filled him once more. They moved cautiously towards each other, as if they were covered in shattered glass, amazed at the force that had ignited.

'It arrives, doesn't it?' she murmured mysteriously, partly to herself.

'It falls.'

'Even when it's not welcome,' Annabel replied.

'The decisions are made in advance. We know what we are going to do and even how we are going to do it.

Sam picked up the tab, opened the door, and went out. Annabel followed him. They got into his car and drove in silence to his house. It occurred immediately. He pushed her against the wall and entered her. She was silent. He carried her to the bedroom, exposing her nakedness and then guiding her arms through the silk pyjama jacket. She surrendered. He buttoned it up slowly, only to undo it again even more slowly. Then he placed his lips on her pink nipples, sucking them slowly. He kissed the round, soft breasts beneath them. Reaching out to the bedside table, he found oil and poured it onto her skin and behind her ears, kissing her entire being as he did so. He was floating high above her, down beneath her, and around her. Her body had an extraordinary fluidity. He watched as she fell into the first orgasmic wave. It was at this point that he entered her. He felt himself expand within her. This took her into a second wave. He stopped and covered her breasts with kisses before pushing further inside her as her back arched. She moaned as he flooded her again and again. It was as if he couldn't stop plunging deep into her, taking possession of her. It had been a long, long time. Now, he released all his pain, all his anguish. His moisture streamed into her. He was powerless to stop this stream, this stream of life-giving fluid, to control the fluid; it saturated her.

It ended suddenly. There was no warning, but it would never have been all right, the ending not being inside this woman – it would never ever again be all right.

He held her tightly. He entered her again. This time, the urge was stronger. He pushed her body into whatever position he wanted and held it there while he entered her. In every way, he felt different; he lengthened inside her and felt like steel. She closed around him, and then he would groan as his moisture poured into her. At these times, he would shake. At other times, he would close round her like a vice, so she felt that she couldn't breathe. Darkness fell when he released her at last. She did not speak.

He left the bed and pulled on his pyjamas. He handed the silk Chanel pyjamas to her and told her to put them on. She didn't move. He went downstairs. When he returned, she still did not speak. He watched her against the pillow, the red hair so thick against her face. He stroked her cheek. She murmured but still there were no words, just a smile. He held the cup for her. She lifted her head to sip the sweet tea, and he saw that her hand was shaking. He grasped it and placed it on his shoulder. Sam made this gesture and felt a healing – something within him healed, something mended.

'Why were you so sad?' he asked at last.

'It's complicated, and it's a long story.'

'Well, I have time to listen.'

Annabel told him the bulk of it.

'Do you want to go back now, to Handford?' Sam asked.

'I just feel that I'm supposed to remain in London for some reason.'

'I see,' he said. He trusted this woman who he hardly knew. There was strength here, as well as passion. 'I want to introduce you to someone this afternoon. She lives not far away from here. Do you mind? It's just that I need to share her. I haven't shared her with anyone, not really.'

'I need time to absorb, to process what's happened. I have to be alone to reintegrate myself, so that I can return to my former life intact, to be complete again.'

'Very well,' he replied.

While Sam made the toast, his emotions swung around in circles, backwards to the night that had passed, forward into the coming week. There was the velvet softness of the night that had passed. He had never felt so tender or so precious. This preciousness was her gift to him, and he knew it had to be protected. He considered how he was going to protect what had been given to him while, at the same time, returning to reality. While these thoughts buzzed around inside his head, he tried to produce a semblance of order. He heard her on the phone to Aveda making an appointment for that afternoon. He knew the plant oils were powerful; they contained their own deep wisdom. They were required right now.

'This is the time for reflection,' she said.

'Why were you crying the other day in Carluccio's?' Sam murmured as he took hold of her hand.

'I was confused. Confusion makes me cry. That's how I react,' she confessed.

'And now?' he asked, as he spread copious amounts of marmalade on his toast.

'I'm more confused, but underneath the confusion there lies a certainty, and it's that certainty I need to discover.'

'I see,' he whispered. 'Last night I felt I was flying.'

'Enough. When there are no words, keep silent,' Annabel said, putting her fingers to his lips as she spoke.

He kissed her, and she left, with no promises and no words.

****

Annabel entered the spa in Westbourne Grove. While she sat in the waiting area, she looked at her mobile, which had been switched off since the evening before. She saw that seven messages had been left for her from Ruth. She quickly threw the phone back into her bag because the therapist had arrived. Annabel said she wanted a massage that was calming, one that would bring her clarity and balance, as well as a soothing facial.

She was led into a darkened room, and invited to smell various aromatherapy essential oils. She told the therapist about her inner turmoil and confusion, and together they chose frankincense, clary sage, and neroli. Annabel smiled, while admitting to the therapist that she was in a personal crisis. This was one of Annabel's great strengths; she realized the importance of looking after herself, no matter what state she found herself in. She had self-awareness. She was in touch with her innermost feelings.

While she was having her massage, her thoughts slowed, and as they slowed, they clarified. She became aware of the enormity of what had occurred. Sam had touched something within her, which, until that point, she was unaware of. Prior to last night, Annabel had never thought of herself as sensual. She'd always thought of herself as adequate, no more than that – at least, in the bedroom and in the looks department. Things were very different now. It was as if she'd flown higher; she was higher in her own estimation. Quite simply, she loved herself. Her self-esteem had grown. She understood, for the first time, the power of her own sexuality. She left the salon two hours later and felt strong enough to answer her mobile messages.

'Hello, it's me.'

'Where on earth have you been? What have you been doing? I thought something had happened to you,' Ruth replied angrily.

'You don't want to know. You really don't. I've spent the afternoon in Aveda, and now I'm at least clearer in my own mind.'

'What are you doing now? Are you coming over?'

'Yes, but tomorrow I have to go back to Hereford. I'll throw myself into my work, certainly until May when my contract comes to an end.'

'Okay, see you soon.'

Annabel knew that she had made the correct decision, and nothing would change her mind. What she had learnt was that she had not missed Geoffrey. There was work to be faced and deficits advice to be given. She was so glad she'd only signed up for one year with the trust instead of three, which is what the board had wanted originally.

Sam phoned later. She told him what she'd decided.

He replied, 'This above all – to thine own self be true, / And it must follow, as the night the day, / Thou canst not then be false to any man.'

CHAPTER THIRTEEN

Judith was went to answer the door of her flat and saw John standing there. She let him in. There was so much invading her head when she saw him that she wanted to sit down and contain her own response.

'My father said you were coming,'

She looked at him and then she looked again. It felt as if he were examining her as an entomologist would examine an insect. She thought immediately of Kafka's *Metamorphosis* and wondered if she resembled one of her own cockroaches. Could this, she wondered, be the reason he was looking at her in the way that he was?

She was worried about infecting him. The climate in family life tends to be one of humility, tolerance, and mutual acceptance. Judith had never known this kind of climate, and so she was incapable of discerning it even when it was quite obviously present. Judith had lost herself. She saw herself now as a lump of meat with teeth and an insatiable appetite for self-annihilation. Something fundamental had changed; the light had gone out.

'How are you? Could you tell me what it's like to be you at this moment? Could you tell me the thought that you have at this precise moment?'

'My nest is ready,' she replied.

'Where is it?'

'In my head, do you want to see my painting?'

John got up and went into the studio. Judith began to laugh as he looked at it.

'Do you like it?'

'It interests me,' he replied.

'Claude and my father loathe it. They want to destroy it.'

'It's unusual.'

'Could you live with it?' she asked.

'Can you?'

'It's mine.'

'It' yours of course it is, very much so.'

'Is that why he's sent you here? To get rid of it, to persuade me to get rid of it,'

'No, it's not. Could we talk about this painting,'

'What do you want?'

'I want to understand your painting. Could you explain it to me?' 'The eyes-birds nests, birds nesting in the eye sockets,'

'Your dreams, are the birds in your dreams. Is this a painting of a dream by any chance?

'No, no not really, I don't know.'

I want you to tell me your dreams.'

'Is that it?'

'Write them down at night – that's all I ask.'

'Okay, if that's really all you want.'

He explained to Judith that the next meeting would be at his flat and left.

Judith suspected that there was something about her that fascinated John. She thought his interest macabre but interesting. She made herself an espresso and sat down to write an account of the vivid dreams she'd experienced the night before.

She accepted without question that sometimes in our lives we encounter people who may, indeed, be strangers but in whom we develop an interest, almost at first sight, without a word being spoken. When he saw her in Provence, she thought it was her beauty that held him, but now she knew that there was something more. She was malnourished; she knew that. She was also withdrawn and miserable. The portrait revealed her true self – what she had become since her return from France. There had been no sign of it at that time. She had unlocked something dark within her; it had revealed her shadow. The painting revealed Judith's psyche through a deep and, at times, disturbing dialogue.

Judith slept that night, and once again, she was jolted awake by shouting, screaming, howling, and cursing. She raised herself up and sat on the bed as the screaming got louder and louder. It was her mother's voice she heard. It turned to no more than a rasp. Judith shook. She heard the voice speaking; its words were almost indistinct because it spoke so rapidly. What on earth was happening? Had the world turned upside down? She fell back onto her bed but couldn't close her eyes.

She'd gone through terror with this creature. Was it in pain? Judith wondered. Was it her? Or was it something manifesting itself within her? It was as though a foreign body had entered her as she lay there on the bed. Then she saw her mother's head materialize, whole and unbroken, beside her. She couldn't move; she couldn't extricate herself from the proximity of this head. She placed her hand on the pillow beside her mother's head, but as she tried to touch it, it disappeared as if it had never been. There was nothing.

She looked around, and in the grey mist of night, her mother stood in front of her, with eye sockets filled with birds' nests exactly like the ones in her painting a laugh that changed to a cackle, and filled the room around then a mocking sound. ... And then, once again, the wailing began, louder than before.

Delirium followed. Heat engulfed her. She was in the grip of a fever. She felt thirsty, but her legs would not move. Her throat had turned to razor blades. Sweat saturated her. There were moments of semi-awareness. Sometimes she felt that there were large numbers of people who wanted to take her away somewhere. There was arguing. The next moment, she was alone in the room; everyone had gone. Then she heard the sound of laughter, mockery even. She remembered Claude, but then he was gone. She couldn't reach him. Sometimes it seemed that she had been lying there for at least a month. At other times, she knew that it was the same night or, at least, a series of nights.

Dawn came, but it was unlike any other dawn. Judith slowly emerged from her bed and drank water and tea in copious amounts. She opened the door to the studio, and there she was – the face on the canvas, this face that had lain next to her own. She picked dramatic colours for her palette, but in some mysterious way, they enslaved her. She was in thrall to them, and they blended together to create their own reality. The face on the canvas was that of her mother bedecked with jewels, the jewels of Desdemona. That face she had created in the previous weeks was altered without warning. The eye sockets still contained the birds' nests as before, but within them were emeralds, tiny emeralds that shimmered in the light.

Judith heard the voice inside her head: *That's better. That's much better.*

She tried to alter it, to remove the emeralds, to paint them out, but her hand would not obey the commands of her mind, and so the tiny emeralds remained. It was as if this painting were filled with a mute spirit, as though this painting had taken on a life of its own and had its own separate existence.

She was very hungry and had been for several hours. It was her day to go out and buy food, but today she could not go. In the past when she'd gone out, the street had been filled with people who knew…she knew… Everyone knew. Judith felt a loathing for everyone she saw, and frequently this feeling turned to deep revulsion. Where, after all, did she belong? What species did she belong to?

Ivy, the cleaner, bought milk and yogurt with her every morning. She could see into the studio from the road. She gingerly opened the door of the studio.

'Hello, Judith I'm making coffee. Do you want some?'

'Yes, please, a big pot. Make it strong,' she replied.

Ivy took in the coffee, but Judith didn't speak. Instead, she grabbed hold of the mug with trembling hands and lifted it slowly, deliberately to her lips. Then she put in three spoonfuls of sugar, which she never did. Judith didn't take sugar.

'Is there anything you want me to do especially?' Ivy asked.

'No nothing,'

Judith's speech was rapid. She was unable to control her breathing, so the words poured out. She left the studio and went into the bedroom where she saw dark red lines on the curtains, as if someone had thrown a pot of paint at them. The sheets were soaking wet, so she threw them hastily into the washing machine but didn't turn it on. She didn't know what stopped her. It was either instinct or intuition – maybe both.

She dialled the number. Sam answered at once, which was unusual for him. 'Hello' he said clearly.

'I don't think things are quite right.'

'I'll be there at once.'

Judith went into the kitchen, found the yogurt that Ivy had brought, and poured lavender honey into it. The flavour and the aroma lighted her memory. She remembered the wonderful house in Provence; the lovemaking with Claude; and, most of all, the crimson sunset. She laughed and took spoonfuls of this deliciousness into her mouth. It gently ran down her chin as she closed her eyes. The memory gently wiped away the hideous night that had passed. Her father arrived.

Oh, there's my darling father, my protector. Have some jam.' She poured it on to his lips and began to lick the sweet nectar from his mouth.

Sam pushed her away onto the chair behind her. She laughed as she fell backwards. He stared at this complete stranger. She looked away, anxious to avoid his gaze. There were red marks on the floor. The bed was unmade. The sheets had disappeared.

'Where are the sheets?' he asked.

'In the washing machine, but I haven't turned it on,' she replied. He dragged the sheets out.

'This is…difficult,' Sam muttered.

'Difficult's what I do,' Ivy replied smiling. 'I don't like dull, and I especially don't like ordinary. That's why I took this job – it's near.'

'Whatever happens from now on, you'll always have work with me.' 'Thanks. That's worth a lot, Mr Bach.' Ivy smiled at him and realized that, in the midst of chaos, a link had been formed. This man, she knew, would always take care of her and her family.

"I think you should come home with me for awhile, Judith'

'That's the last place on earth I want to be! Home with you is the last place I want to be,' she shouted.

'Why is that?'

'No, no, no. This is my home.'

'You need to feel safe. You don't feel safe, do you?' Sam enquired . 'Why the hell are you being so bloody nice? It's all a bit late. You know that,' Judith replied bitterly.

'I've made mistakes, I know. Perhaps I should have got rid of her somehow – divorced her, left her somewhere, taken you abroad, sent you away to boarding school. I didn't know what to do. After Harry died, she changed. She was grief-stricken. I was sorry for her. Right up to the end, I was sorry for her. I did try to get her treatment, but it was no good. It just didn't bloody well work. I had so much to learn after your grandfather died, and I was very young. Why can't you see it from my point of view? You're not a child any more.'

'It's all too late, much too late.'

'I tried to make it up to you by giving you this flat. I pay Ivy. I buy your pictures when no one else will!' Sam yelled.

'You left me with her, when you knew she was too drunk to stand up. You left her to take care of me, take care of me, when she couldn't stand up. No, I'll never come home to…'

'What?'

'I'll never ever come home, Dad. I'll never come home again.'

'I don't understand.'

'It's impossible.'

Silence fell between them. Sam embraced his daughter and left. She loved his embrace. Despite herself, she loved his touch. She always had done, but now there was a distance between them. She thought how cold it was, how impossible it was to make things right.

Forgiveness… She watched from the window and observed his gait, fast and furious. She sensed that something fundamental had altered within him. It was as if he were trying to walk away, not just from her but from himself.

Chapter Fourteen

Something had changed within Judith; restlessness, a need, had emerged from deep within her psyche. It moved around in monstrous form, eventually settling in her soul. She realized that, despite all her efforts to destroy it, this need had found a suitable corner. At times, it lay dormant, but at other times it roared.

She imagined telling John Antony about the other night. She also wanted to tell him that the dream had recurred again. The dream followed on from the night where she had seen the haunting, the face on the pillow. Ideas of personal annihilation had followed, but there were doubts, fears that the head would be there. It might lie beside her in the coffin waiting…as it had been on the pillow. It might be in the grave. It could, in fact, be anywhere. She'd seen it now in so many places; it was as if it lay in wait for her. There was no guarantee that it would release her after death, so annihilation lost its appeal. She wondered if there was anywhere it would not be when she heard it roa. She looked around to see if she could locate it, but that was always fruitless.

This phenomenon was jealous. It roared if she was with anyone. She heard it loudly when she and Claude spent the night together. Passion always awakened it. The roaring was so loud and so hideous that she asked him to go; when he refused, she threw him out into the street.

He sent her a letter. She opened it and read it.

Dearest Judith,

It's a long time since I wrote a letter. Maybe it's a long time since you read one. This is not an email, it's not a text – it's a letter. I'm not even sure where to begin or even if I want it to end, and most of me doesn't want it to end.

The glorious day in Provence. It was in that garden. You clambered out of your vehicle, clutching two or three canvases and an easel. It wasn't merely that you were beautiful; it was the sheer loveliness that captured me and held me entranced, that day and every day since. There was also your work, the paintings you showed me of the olive trees growing among the gravestones and all those shades of green. I believe you said you mixed one hundred and one shades of green to create that extraordinary picture. It still haunts me to this day. Often now, when I close my eyes, I see you holding this in your hands. Other nights, I see your nakedness and remember how wonderful it was to hold you close to me on those balmy summer nights. However, those memories belong to a past time and a past place.

Something extraordinary has happened; you have changed. The Judith who mixed one hundred and one shades of green is no more, and I do miss her so. Something profound has happened to you – you are changed. I'm angry with you because there is no explanation. And because there is no explanation there can be no understanding. You are the person I love most in the world. The person I love is altered. We committed ourselves to one another when we were in France. It wasn't just a holiday romance. We held hands on the boat as we crossed the sea. I watched your long hair blowing in the wind, and I knew I'd found what I'd searched for all my life. Now, I visit you but you're not there any more. The Judith I knew has been taken from me. The beautiful black hair has gone; you've had it all cut off. Your face is different; your skin has lost both its colour and its luminosity. Are you ill? If you are, then why can't you tell me? Your paintings were so full of light and colour – all that has gone.

This is all I have to say. I have to know what is wrong, or it is the end.

Claude

In the morning, after she had read the letter, she went into the studio and placed it on the table next to her palette knife. She'd slept a bit that night. It had been quieter. She had tossed and turned, but it was perfect, as it should have been – or so she felt. She began to paint. The face looked smoother, sharper than before. She worked silently on the jawline. There was a symbiosis. She saw, once again, her mother's face emerge as if through veils of gossamer, until it merged eventually with her own. The question arose as to whether it was her self-portrait or a painting of her mother. Judith didn't know. The tiny birds' nests within the eye socket extended to the brow line. The forehead she daubed with thick heavy lumps of white. Then she picked up a tube of dove grey, and with her smallest palette knife, she placed tiny dots of this grey on the white. This task took several hours. Her consciousness was aware only of this process of grey-on-white mingling. It mesmerized her. She was held by the process – white on grey, grey on white…on and on it went.

The cleaner put her head through to enquire whether or not she was going to have some breakfast. Judith moved into the kitchen.

'Your letter, I saw it when I arrived this morning. Do you want it?'

Judith's nightdress was covered with paint. 'I've read it,' she replied, pouring some blackberry jam into a huge bowl of yogurt.

She read it once more and then again. As she read it, her throat contracted. Her mouth felt dry, dusty almost. She got up from the table, walked to her bedroom, and dragged some clothes out of the wardrobe – a thick baggy sweater and some woollen leggings. She put them on and sat at the dressing table, where she found face cream. She massaged it into her face and her neck, trying to calm herself. Fear rose within her. She applied layers of black mascara. The movement of her lashes against the brush held her away from dark despair. She thought of the day she'd bought it – that day, that day in Harvey Nichols. She found the rouge noir lipstick and drew a line around the contours of her lips, applying several layers, smudging each with a tissue. This mouth matched her nails; this deep dark red contrasted with her grey eyeshadow. Alabaster face powder finished the look; there was something of the gothic about her.

'I'm going out!' she shouted to Ivy.

She crumpled up the letter and almost ran to John Antony's flat. She knocked on the door. John answered it.

'Judith, you're very early,' he said.

It was as if she hadn't heard what he'd said. She held the letter out towards him. Her hands trembled. She could not dislodge this feeling even for a moment. She realized her mistake. He was too close to

Claude. He'd known him too long and travelled down too many paths with him, paths which had, at times, proved dangerous, treacherous even. She understood suddenly that this was the reason for the empathy he felt towards her; it was contagious and had travelled in some mysterious form.

'I hear sounds like howling, screaming, and screeching and then wake up and see a head on my pillow, a head that's been beheaded.'

'What does that make you feel,'

'Screaming,'

'Describe the scream.'

'Loud.'

'How loud?'

'Howling.'

'Like what?'

'Me,' she replied, playing with the ring on her right hand.

'You?'

'Me.'

'Howling, like you?' John replied.

'Yes.'

'Are you howling?'

'Yes, inside I'm howling,' she whispered.

'Go back. Describe the head.'

'I can't. It's impossible.'

She would then be giving it both reality and life.

'Is it your head…in the dream?'

'No, it's not mine. It's not my head,' she said emphatically.

'Do you recognize it?'

'The head?'

Yes.'

'What occurs?'

'The head laughs, howls, screams, and then vanishes. I look at the pillow and find that it's vanished. I... She was there, but she...'

'Vanishes,' John murmured.

'Yes.'

'How does that feel?'

'Like...as if my chest is going to burst, and I'll never reclaim it.'

'Reclaim what, Judith?'

She looked, at that moment, like a caged animal wanting to break free. Her eyes moved around the room, seeing all the ancient books that lined the walls. It was as if they were moving around from place to place.

'Nothing is still,' she murmured.

'No.'

'Even the books have their seasons and their moments. They too have a time when they're born.'

'You were born, Judith. Someone made it possible for you to exist,' John said.

You're so clever,'

'You, Judith, were the person who mentioned birth. Not me – you.' 'The books made me think of birth; that's all. They just made me feel...cocooned. It's like a cocoon, this place. Womb-like,'

'How does womb-like feel?'

'Contained and held. When you are in the womb you are protected.' 'Is that good, to feel like that? A pre-birth state?'

'You made me mention birth.'

'No,' John replied.

'You think...it's about her,'

'I have no idea what this is about, I know you're troubled that's what I know. That is all I know.'

'My father told me to come here. I want to go home now.'

'You are free to leave.'

'Do you want me to stay here with you in this warm cocoon, away from everyone and everything? It's soporific.'

Judith felt safe and warm in this room. She noticed the old, golden carpet on the floor and the gentle smell of cardamom mixed with leather. Some winter potpourri sat on the table. She didn't want to leave. She would never want to leave because out there was chaos. Her mother was out there. She wasn't in here.

'I want you to stay until the end of the session.'

Judith began to cry. 'It's...not safe,'

'Safe, let's stay right here. What's not safe?'

'Out there, out there, in here,' she said, pointing at her head.

'We are going to do something called free association. I will say words to you, and you will say what comes into your head immediately.'

'Olive,' he said.

'Paint.'

'Bruise.'

'Me.'

'Enter.'

'Mother,' she replied.

'Milk.'

'Mother.'

'Blue,' he said.

'Death.'

'Desire.'

'Dawn.'

'Closure.'

'My olive trees, they've gone away.'

'When did they go?' John murmured.

'The day you saw me in the street. I've never seen them since.'

'Why that day? Why do you think they went that day in particular?' he asked.

Judith hesitated. She didn't answer.

'Did something happen on that day?'

'One day, they disappeared. I've never seen them since.'

'Where? Where did you see them?'

'I used to see them in my head, but they've vanished. They were beautiful. I loved them, but now they've left me.'

'Judith, when did they leave?'

She didn't answer for a long time. She thought about them. She saw them all gnarled and broken. Where once there had been leaves, there were, instead, tiny shrunken heads.

'One day,' she whispered.

'What happened on that day?'

'Nothing.'

'Go on.'

'She gave me life. Thus, she is the only thing that matters – the beginning and the end.

'No, it's the process that matters – like a painting.'

A hammering at the front door of the flat broke the silence. At first, John ignored it, but it got louder and more insistent.

'I'm going to have to answer the door,' he said.

Sam burst in. 'Why didn't you tell me you'd seen her?' he shouted. John didn't answer but returned to his chair.

Judith tried to run out of the flat, but Sam threw her back into the room.

'I've been to Harvey Nichols. My American Express receipt said you'd shopped in this shop on the day your mother died the woman at the cosmetic counter knows me it's where I'd go when I wanted perfume for your mother. I showed her the receipt and she said she remembered you because few people bought 'rouge noir' as many people find it too dark. She said you were very strange,'

Judith didn't reply for a long time, eventually she said she'd forgotten. 'I don't believe you. I simply don't believe you! You're lying!' Sam roared.

Judith curled up in her chair, she whimpered.

'You should have told me,' Sam said looking directly at John.

'It was difficult. You asked me to see Judith in a professional capacity, and she had already asked me to tell no one. That's why I said nothing, 'John replied.

'I never knew you loved her. I didn't know you loved her. Why did you have to love her? She was a drunk. She was vile. But you had to love her, didn't you? Why didn't you take me away from her, leave her, divorce her – anything? But no, you just stayed and stayed and stayed. To stay – that was always your mantra. You could always escape to work. Never mind if she left me in the cupboard without food, without water, unable to escape. I was so frightened I used to wet myself. I wanted to be with you. But no, you didn't want that. I wanted to be with you.'

'What happened, Judith? Tell me what happened,'Sam said softly

'You happened. Mum happened. And then I happened. How could you have a child with someone like that? How could you?'

'She wasn't like that when I met her. I've explained to you. After Harry died, she changed; she never got over Harry's death. She loved him so much she couldn't recover. No one could reach her.'

'Claude told me about…van Gogh's mother…the mourning mother syndrome. I was never good enough. She wanted something, someone else – not me.' A tear fell from her eye.

'You weren't good enough,' John repeated.

'No. She wanted him. She wanted Harry. She never wanted me.'

'She never wanted you?'

'She wanted Harry. It was as if it were my fault he'd died.'

'Your fault?'

Sam sat silently, gazing at his hands. He couldn't look at his daughter.

A possibility had entered his head, a possibility so shocking that he could scarcely take it in – so he gazed into space. And it was no ordinary space but as huge and incomprehensible as the universe itself.

'Yes, my fault,' she whispered.

Judith looked away from both men. Suddenly, she picked up the letter from the edge of the table and passed it to her father. He read it slowly and replaced it on the table. Silence soaked the air, allowing imagination to travel.

It led John down strange alleyways. He saw in his mind's eye the letter with four stones, one on each corner. He got up from his chair and reached for a dark rosewood box he'd bought many years ago when travelling in Tibet. Inside it was a selection of small precious stones that he'd collected over the years. He passed the box to Judith and asked her to choose two out of the box. She held her hand over the lovely stones for a few moments and then placed two lumps of lapis lazuli on two of the four corners of the letter. John passed the box to Sam, and he chose two lumps of amethyst. The three sat silently as the early evening light receded. John drew the faded velvet curtains and turned on a couple of lamps, which cast a soft light across the room, reminiscent of candlelight.

'You haven't put a stone on the page,' Judith said.

'I've saved the best until last,' he replied. With that, he reached into the box and found a tiny, dark ruby. John placed it right in the centre of the paper and stared at Judith as the soft light reflected on the stone, transforming it into a drop of blood. Judith stared at it.

She did as John asked her to and drew a perfectly straight line across the page. It passed by the side of the tiny red ruby and joined her piece of lapis lazuli to her father's amethyst.

'What are you thinking about now, at this moment?' John asked Sam.

'I'm thinking of venous blood flowing through veins.'

'What's in your mind now, Judith, at this moment?'

'Blood, on the letter,' Judith replied.

'Anything else about the letter, anything particular, any words or phrases?'

'The man who wrote it.'

'Claude

'Of course. Who else could it be?' she murmured.

'Is there anything you'd like to say to him?' John asked.

'What can I say? What is there to say?' she replied.

'You loved him once.'

'I love him now.'

'What's changed then?'

'I'm now a murderer. Who would want a murderer in their bed, at their table, in their house? No one, no one at all.' Flowers and flames merged in her mind as she spoke.

Sam looked at her in the way that one person looks at another when the words they are uttering untie the bonds that bind them.

Judith looked at her father's face. For a moment, her eyes held his, and in that second, a new reality was born, a reality she could never have imagined. Now she was alone. She had crossed the Rubicon, and there was no pathway by which she could return to the place she had occupied in her father's heart since the day she was born. She knew the isolation of the dispossessed. The feeling grew; it crawled around her, filling every crevice of her mind, every sinew of her heart, every pore of her skin. It was metamorphosis.

The air that I breathe will never be the same, she thought. The aromas that I smell will never be as they once were, for I am not as I once was. This conviction, this realization, changed the colour of her face, the temperature of her hands, and the speed of her heart rate.

John held the silence between these two people. They were tiptoeing into another reality where neither had a guide. A vision of a desert entered his consciousness, a desert without an oasis. There were no camels in this place to bring the travellers to safety. For most surely there was no safety here, no water, no nourishment.

'You killed her. You killed her,' Sam whispered.

'Yes, I killed her.'

'Your own mother.'

Judith didn't answer. She went into her own being, which was now a foreign land without signposts.

'Why? Why? For God's sake, why?'

'Why not?' she replied.

Sam left the room; the flat; and, finally, himself.

'I suppose you don't want to see me anymore,' Judith murmured to John.

'I want you to go home now and live in the dreamworld. When you go to sleep, take a pen and paper with you and write down any dreams you may have had. Return here in forty-eight hours. If you feel unsafe, then ring me. Don't ring anyone else for the time being.'

She left and walked slowly through the cold, ice-bound London streets. When she reached home, the flat was in darkness. She wandered into the studio and looked at the painting. It terrified her. She shut the door. She went to bed, to sleep, and stayed there immersed in her own thoughts and dreams, which centred on a cold, empty lake. There was nothing but water, water that didn't move. Her mother appeared, dressed in a long white gown. Then she entered the water and immersed herself, as if in baptism.

Judith woke and looked around. She saw her mother's face in the mirror of her dressing table. She heard a laugh, and then another, a mocking sound that reached out into the night, into the blackness. There was only blackness. Judith wrapped her duvet round and round her body, half awake and half asleep. Visions appeared that dissolved into dreams and then into nightmares, where she walked frail and downtrodden, wandering on from land to land.

When she awoke she wondered, *How can this be the person that I thought was my own flesh and blood, the root of my soul, the origin of my being, the first sound that I heard, the first food that I ate? How can this be, and what now of me? Is there a me? There is no me, not now. There is no me.* She tossed and turned and lay there half awake, half asleep, in a kind of no man's land.

Forty-eight hours later, she found herself back at John Antony's flat, which was unaltered since the last visit. Judith found this comforting. He also was unchanged. He was constant.

'Did you dream?' John Antony asked.

'Yes, I wrote it down as you instructed, at least some of it. To write down all of it, record all of it, would take a lifetime. So I'll tell you as much as I can. She seemed to be wandering around in my flat. I saw her in the mirror. I saw her face,' she replied.

'Go on.'

'I find myself wandering about in a part of London I don't know.

It's a very strange, mysterious area full of dead trees in various stages of decomposition. I feel drawn towards it. I walk through it. There are footpaths everywhere, and yet I have a sense that it's deserted, and no one has been there for a long time. It looks as if the trees are saturated with water, and that's why they are dead. I love it here. I have no idea why, but it's the place I want to be. Maybe it's the place I've searched for all my life. It's a relief to be away from all that interminable beauty. … This is my land. I may not know it, but it's mine. Suddenly, in my path I see a hand, sticking out from beneath the earth. There's a ring on every finger, and the flesh is rotten. I start to dig with my hands. I'm curious. The digging becomes frantic, as if I'm digging for my life. A head emerges, at least a skull and decomposing skin. The eyes have gone. There remain two holes, occipital bones. I begin to cry, but there is no one there. I shout at the corpse, "Who are you? What are you doing there? Who the hell are you?" I find a handbag that's full of precious stones. It's hardly disintegrated at all.'

'The corpse is the only thing that matters,' whispered John,

Judith looked at him. She ran her fingers through her hair while shaking her head.

'The corpse is the only thing. There's nothing else in my life. It's there always, no matter where I go, no matter what I do.'

'How long has it been the only thing that matters?'

'Since the day she died, there has been nothing…nothing else.'

'Are you afraid?'

'I'm afraid.'

'When?'

'Always.'

'What is the fear?'

'We are not divided any more. Before, we were separate defined beings.

We inhabited different skins. We had separate thoughts, separate minds. Now we are one.'

'As in alchemy,' John whispered.

'The alchemy of murder – the murdered and the murderer,' Judith whispered.

'Go on.'

'We are joined now, indivisible.'

'You are inseparable?'

'The dream place, the place I visited…' 'You are trying to rescue her.'

'Resurrect her.'

'Do you want her resurrected?'

'Rescued.'

'You want her rescued?'

'I always wanted her rescued, but no one could rescue her, you see. No one could rescue her. My father tried to rescue her.'

'In your dream you're digging her up. That's one form of rescue. You're rescuing her from decomposition.'

'She's decomposed. In my dream, she's already decomposed.'

'But you're digging, aren't you?'

'Yes, I'm digging,' Judith replied.

The session over, John Anthony said he wanted her to continue with her dream diary and to return to see him the next day.

****

Judith walked home through the damp and dismal streets of west London. It rained heavily. And by the time she got home, she was soaked. She glanced into the studio, but hastily closed the door behind her.

The painting. How can I get rid of it? she thought.

Miss Dyne...she would ask her to come over and then they could discuss it. Judith had been a student at the Royal Academy with Mary Dyne, who was ferociously talented. She would give her an accurate appraisal and advise her on galleries where she would be most likely to find a buyer. There was, of course, far more to it than that. She loved Mary Dyne and wanted her comfort. She found the number on her mobile, and there she was – a voice. The sound of this friend was like the caress of a warm air current.

'I wonder if you could come over and see me? I have a painting I'd like you to see.'

'Of course. I have a free evening, so I could come and see you tonight, if that's all right?'

'It's fine,' she said rapidly.

'I'll be there at seven thirty.'

Judith put down the phone. She sat still, waiting, and wondering whether it was time to get rid of the painting. She didn't know, but then she didn't know anything. No one liked the painting. Everyone who saw it looked away in horror.

Why? Is that why? Does it matter that much if no one likes it? Maybe it does...but perhaps not. It depends on the way it looks she thought of van Gogh, who couldn't even give his paintings away.

Mary Dyne arrived at the time she's said she would. Judith felt warmed by her mere presence. She led her into the studio, and there she sat, just gazing at it. For some time, she said nothing. Mary Dyne looked at it from many angles.

'It is…'

'It is what, Mary?'

'Unique. It's utterly unique. And it reminds me of many different styles, many different painters. Somehow, they're fused together. Bacon is the one that comes immediately to mind – the image overlaid with the beautiful colouring.'

'I don't know how to paint the way I used to paint. It's as if…old certainties have gone, only to be replaced by something alien.' Judith trembled as she spoke.

Mary Dyne looked at Judith. She noticed the amount of weight she had lost and the lacklustre look in her eyes. She remembered her the last time they'd met, a couple of years earlier. She was unable to respond, unable to match up the Judith of now with the earlier one.

'Do you know of any gallery that might take it away for me?'

'Yes, I know one or two good ones that I could recommend – if that's what you want?'

'I need to dispose of it, to free myself.'

'With this painting you have joined the surrealist movement,' Mary replied, 'that surprises me I would never have thought it of you. It is in many ways a very fine painting indeed.'

'People who see it are disturbed by it-do you think it hideous?'

'No of course I don't know more than I consider Bacon to be hideous.'

CHAPTER FIFTEEN

Annabel thought about Sam and how he was, but, being Annabel, she settled into that element of her work that she enjoyed most – the decisions that had to be made regarding deficit reduction in individual departments. She enjoyed it particularly because of its inherent complexity. It took up all her thought processes, and so there was little time for anything else.

She was having particular difficulty with the intensive care department and with considering the implications involved in keeping one person alive. She had to consider, almost on a daily basis, the monetary value of one human life. The specialists, doctors, nurses, and consultants on that particular unit all believed that human life is impossible to quantify in terms of money. They were intractable and impossible to reason with in any way. She felt that their blatant hostility to all suggestions of financial reduction was unreasonable. Part of her admired their tenacity, but another part of her despised it.

One day, she'd had a particularly hostile meeting with the head of the department, in which she'd proposed closing two beds instead of one. This idea followed the release of a monthly figure revealing that the deficit had increased, despite reducing the facilities in the addiction unit. These setbacks only served to make Annabel more determined than ever, and when she was in this kind of mood, she could be ruthless. The conversations that took place in her office became more and more confrontational. Many were seen leaving her office in tears, as further precious hospital facilities were suggested to the trust as areas where cuts could be made. She was determined to find methods to reduce the deficit one way or another; that was her job. She was hated and feared by most members of the staff, as they all realized their own departments would be targeted. It was a lonely existence.

She worked tirelessly day after day and seemed impervious to her body's need for either rest or relaxation.

Ruth phoned to remind her that Christmas was fast approaching. 'Hello, how are you?'

'I'm working. That's how I am.'

'Any other news?' Ruth asked.

'No. I'm busy.'

Ruth immediately sensed her sister's work voice, and she knew well that there was little point in continuing the conversation in that vein, so she immediately changed tack.

'What about Christmas? Are you coming to us? We love it when you come to us; you know that. We haven't seen you for ages, or so it seems.'

'You need to go back to work, Ruth. It would expand your horizons. It does that for everyone,' Annabel muttered with exasperation.

'If you want to know, I'm working two days a week at the hair salon where I started my training. Some of my old mates are still there.'

'Thank God for that. The training cost a fortune, and it went on for three years. I used to wonder how on earth it could take three bloody years to learn to cut someone's hair.'

'Why are you being so horrible? We can't all go to university and get a first,' Ruth murmured. She hated it when her sister was like this.

'I'm sorry. I'm tired and irritable.'

'You've no idea how much you have to learn, or you wouldn't be so scathing.'

'I'm not feeling great right now. There's a lot of pressure.'

'Have you seen Geoffrey?'

'Of course I have.'

'What about a Christmas shop?' Ruth said.

'Not now, not at the moment. I'm too busy.'

'Well, it's only three weeks to Christmas. You do realize that, don't you?' 'Three weeks to shop on the Internet is an eternity. In fact, it's a lifetime.'

'Okay. You stuff your nose into your bloody work, just like Alex. He's in New York at some legal thing or other. He's suggested that I go over with the kids for Christmas. I think he wants me to get a job over there, but I don't want to. I want to talk to you. Everyone's so damn busy all the time.'

That's life,' Annabel replied, putting down the phone.

The phone rang again, and then it stopped. There was so much to do. Annabel went through one more draft of figures before running her bath. She lay in it for over an hour, and then she wrapped herself in a huge bathrobe and fell into bed. She slept straightaway, only to be woken at 1 a.m. by the telephone. Drowsily, she opened her eyes and answered the phone.

No one was there. Then it rang again. It was Sam. He wanted to know if she'd be coming up for Christmas. Annabel tried to go back to sleep. She tossed and turned, thinking about what to do. Feelings confused her. She didn't understand this aspect of herself, and because she didn't understand it, she was afraid. She buried this fear in work, knowing how to get from where she was to where she wanted to be. Emotions had a life and a logic all of their own, and that was why they frightened her. She just didn't understand them.

As 6 a.m. arrived, Annabel felt sick. She went to the bathroom and vomited all over the floor. She looked at the mess in horror, knowing that she would have to clean it all up herself. She hated mess, vomit, and being ill. She considered ringing up and saying that she was unwell but dismissed the idea as ludicrous. She had an important meeting that day, and she knew that her non-arrival would be construed as weakness.

It was cold outside. She could see the icicles on the ledge outside her flat. She put on her favourite bra, wondering if it was feeling a bit tight and then a woollen pair of tights and the scarlet dress that always gave her confidence. She'd bought it on one of those many occasions when she felt lonely, when Claude was sad. She'd gone off that day, promising to buy herself something wonderful. And there it had been, displayed in all its glory in a window in Westbourne Grove. It had a beautiful line. Made of a silk and linen mixture, this dress didn't move – it floated. This would be the battledress she'd wear today. Oh, how she loved it, even now.

She rammed some toast into the toaster and spread it with apricot jam. After a couple of mouthfuls, waves of nausea washed over her, and within seconds, she vomited over her much-loved dress. She burst into tears, and her newly applied mascara ran down her face. She cleaned it up, realizing that she would be late for the meeting. She applied her make-up once more, and then she found a clean trouser suit in her wardrobe and put it on. She looked in the mirror and thought how much of a power suit it was and how assertive she looked in it. She found her highest heels in the back of the cupboard. They were for moments such as these – when she had to appear strong and powerful, but felt weak. She'd given up caring by this stage.

She slammed the door of her flat and ran downstairs to her car. She drove somewhat recklessly through the streets of Hereford and arrived bang on time for her meeting.

'How the hell did I do that?' she asked herself. 'I'm bloody amazing, that's what I am.'

The meeting was long and arduous. It involved tenders for the catering. Annabel and the head of catering examined a tender that was considerably cheaper than the one the hospital was using at present. There seemed to be a greater number of vegetarian options and less meat. The puddings, by and large, seemed healthy, if a little dull.

Does hospital food have to be imaginative? Annabel asked herself. The head of catering thought so; Annabel didn't. It was the meat that really caused controversy. The hospital nutritionist thought that a vegetarian option was just as healthy as one containing meat, but the head of catering disagreed. This, Annabel thought, was decidedly dull. She felt uncomfortable, and the meeting dragged on, with the group looking at piles of menus and trying to balance cost with nutritional needs.

It ended at lunchtime with the proposed tender being accepted. This would save the trust thousands of pounds every year. It was a success as far as Annabel was concerned. Annabel ate a sandwich in her office.

The phone went, and it was Geoffrey.

'Hello, Annabel,' he said.

She had an odd feeling. Was it her heart sinking?

'Look, can't we meet? I've hardly seen you at all lately. Could we have dinner tonight?'

Annabel hesitated. She didn't know what to say. She'd been trying to avoid him so that she could get her head straight, but it was anything but straight. It felt like cotton wool, and she still had another meeting in the afternoon with the auditors that she knew would be confrontational because the deficit had not reduced despite the various changes she'd already implemented. It was the bill for the agency nurses that were to blame.

'I have a meeting with the auditors this afternoon,' she replied.

'Poor you. We could eat at the Castle Hotel. It's accessible, it's easy to park there, and the food is good.'

'Yes, that would be nice,' Annabel replied reluctantly.

'What time shall I pick you up?'

'Seven thirty.'

'Very well, see you then.'

She went to the meeting with the auditors, which was scheduled for 2 p.m. She was early enough to get her presentation and her argument in some sort of order before they arrived.

Oh God, she thought, supposing it all gets out of hand and they just throw figures in my direction. I can't argue with their figures. The deficit just won't budge, not with this hefty bill for agency nurses. The only realistic option is to close a theatre or cut one ITU bed, ideally both, and cut down the admissions to the addiction unit.

****

A large auditor arrived with two smaller ones. Annabel put her presentation graph on the projector. It showed clearly the areas where money had been saved within the various departments. The large auditor remarked that the overall budget deficit was no less than it had been when she'd arrived.

She explained in minute detail where the budget for agency staff had gone and admitted that a lot of it had gone on ITU because these nurses were highly skilled and, therefore, expensive. This expense was inevitable unless one of the beds was cut. The inevitable political backlash was discussed and the value of a life – how much is a human life worth in terms of hard currency? This question, they knew, would be hurled at the trust from every quarter. The auditors pondered at great length, over pots of tea, the option of closing one of the theatres. Biscuits were avoided for the sake of frugality.

Eventually, it was agreed that a meeting with the trust would have to be brought forward. The auditors insisted that it had to take place before Christmas. That gave a window of two weeks to prepare. Annabel realized the huge amount of work she was going to have to do for this meeting, which was, in effect, to decide the future of the theatre suite and ITU. At last, the meeting came to an end. Annabel rushed out to her car. The tiny clock on the dashboard said 6.10 p.m. as she sped out of the car park. The town was quiet. She arrived home at 6.15, with an hour to get ready. She had a shower and made herself a coffee.

Oh, my God, she thought, *what am I to do?* She really didn't know what to do. Suddenly, sitting there with the hairdryer for company, she missed *Sam. Why don't I know? Other people know these things – why don't I know?* She was, as is so often the case, angry with herself, frustrated that she didn't know.

Geoffrey was coming in a quarter of an hour. She applied some foundation, Lancome's newest – 'Miracle'. It was the name that had persuaded her to buy it.

I need a bloody miracle. A brain transplant, that's what I need, she thought to herself. *Now stop crying. Imagine what Geoffrey'll think if you're sobbing when he arrives.* She blew her nose and decided against mascara – it was just too risky. The bell rang. She squirted some perfume over her ample bosom and answered the door.

He was standing there. He smiled but said nothing. While they drove to the restaurant, Annabel became convinced that he knew about Sam. She hardly noticed the elegant decor in the restaurant and immediately picked up the menu. She studied it in earnest, eventually deciding on the venison casserole with mashed potatoes, cabbage, and carrots. This was comfort food at its best. It was the perfect choice for Annabel on that day and at that time.

'You're quiet tonight,' Geoffrey remarked.

'I've had a very busy day.'

'Yes, so have I.'

'We're busy people,' Annabel murmured.

Geoffrey looked as glum as Annabel felt.

'Is there anything we can do?' Geoffrey asked.

'To mend it?'

'Do we want to mend it?'

'I don't know.'

'There's nothing to mend. There never was. Accidents happen,' she whispered.

The whole meal had turned into a disaster, and she was at a loss to know what to say. This sort of thing frightened and confused her.

The waiter arrived with the menu for dessert. Annabel, once again, diverted her attention to the matter of choice. Definitely not jam roly-poly or Christmas pudding. She settled, in the end, for damson crumble.

'This is divine,' she said as she took the first mouthful.

'The love never came, I'm afraid,' Geoffrey murmured.

'No, it never did.'

Annabel helped herself to more custard before passing it back to Geoffrey.

'I don't know what to say.'

'It's not simple; it's not simple at all. Why does everyone think everything is simple?' she replied.

'It was simple... Then it became complicated.'

'Nothing is ever simple. We believe things are simple, we tell ourselves they're simple, but they're not.'

''You wouldn't tell me the truth.'

'What is truth? I don't know what truth is,' Annabel said.

'Honesty...we just have to be honest; that's all.'

'Truth is honesty, is it?

'What do you think?' Geoffrey murmured.

'I don't know. I've told you I don't know – anything.'

'It's a cop-out, a way of avoiding what you can't face.'

This remark prompted Annabel to order a large brandy. She downed it in one and promptly ordered another.

'I'm sorry,' she murmured.

Geoffrey didn't answer. He got out his wallet, paid the bill, and walked swiftly out of the restaurant, he waited in his car for Annabel before driving her home.

****

December was one of the coldest on record. Annabel restricted her movements to going between the hospital and her flat. She made the apartment warm and cosy, cheering herself up with faux fur throws and lovely thick bathrobes, which she could wrap herself up in. She drank mugs of hot chocolate and Horlicks and ate hearty vegetable soup. She bought books – no, she didn't have a Kindle. She despised them. How could you possibly snuggle up in bed with a Kindle? The idea was ridiculous. She discovered, that winter, Simon Mawr's The Glass Room. He took her into his own world, an intriguing world. Every evening, she fell asleep with this book in her hands; every morning it was to be found snuggled up where Annabel had dropped it. External relationships became unnecessary. She sent all her friends candles, which she ordered on the Internet. The White company even gift-wrapped them for her. She ordered plenty for herself too, so her flat was filled with the scent of winter – cardamom, cloves, and cinnamon. This was the obsessive Annabel; she created a gorgeous living space for herself, and then worked and worked until the task was accomplished. It was this ability that had gotten her a first at university; she was not only extremely clever but also obsessional when it came to her work.

She endured endless conversations with doctors, ward managers, and senior nurses. Then, of course, there was the media furore at the possibility of a theatre closure. On these cold, lonely winter days she returned to her cosy flat in the evening and worked hour after hour on her laptop, devising five-year projections. She then collapsed into the bath and went to bed. The final hour of every day was spent reading and rereading reports, while her mobile phone recharged itself on the table beside her.

Eventually, however, Annabel succumbed to the demands of her body and went to the doctor. She described the ongoing nausea and vomiting in vivid terms, in the way that only Annabel could, so that the doctor was left in no doubt about the gravity of it. He put it down, at first, to the pressure of work. But Annabel said her life had been like this many times before, and the problem had not arisen then. Blood tests were taken, and she made an appointment to see him the following week for the results. He offered her one-week's sick leave, which she gladly accepted.

It would give her a full week to concentrate on the presentation she was to give to the trust and to contemplate one of the matters that she knew would trouble the trust most. She intended to propose at the meeting that there was a clear choice to be made if the deficit was to be reduced – either one of the theatres would have to close or the number of ITU beds would have to halved. Drastic reductions to the addiction unit were also inevitable. She had looked closely at every other option, but apart from ward closures nothing else would save enough money, especially if chemotherapy drugs were still to be prescribed in order to prolong life by a few years. These drugs had become increasingly expensive, as had the drugs to halt the progress of Alzheimer's. It really was a choice she realized, between the many and the few. There was no painless way to reduce the deficit; there never had been, and there never would be.

During her week's sickness, Sam phoned. Her delight surprised her. He sounded strange, like a traveller who had lost his way on a dark night and wanted to know the best way to go. He wasn't clear. He said it was foggy in London. She said it was cold in Handford. The main purpose of his call was to discover her plans for Christmas – whether was she going to stay in Handford or go to London.

'What are you doing?' he asked.

'I'm so busy at work. I've no time to think about anything else. My head is full of deficits.'

'When does your break start?'

'December the twenty-first. We have a week of meetings before that.

I have two weeks, so I come back on the fourth of January,' she answered.

There was a long silence before he said, 'I'm sorry. I shouldn't have phoned. I...just wanted to...' He put the phone down. A text then appeared on her mobile, asking her to meet him.

Annabel didn't reply at once. She felt lousy from the nausea and the sickness. People said it was simple, but nothing was simple. She had no friends she could phone, not in Handford. Deficit reduction doesn't bring lots of friends with it, but it does bring a pile of enemies. She could ring mates from her days at university, or she could book a massage. The latter was the simplest option, so Annabel, being Annabel, took it.

While she was there, she relaxed as the aroma of rose and geranium oils soothed her. The deficits magically disappeared from consciousness. She thought of Sam. It seemed as though these plant oils were clearing a pathway straight to Annabel's heart, and the weeds of guilt and responsibility were cleared away. She stopped wondering what to do. She determined there and then to phone Sam and go to London for Christmas. The thought of going to the doctor frightened her.

Why didn't she do what she wanted to do? What was stopping her? Could it be some instinct that warned her of danger? She could phone him there and then, invite him down, indulge in uninterrupted lovemaking. No, if she did that, she would lose focus, and she needed focus. Deficits need focus.

CHAPTER SIXTEEN

Meanwhile, Sam's mind used various devices to prevent disintegration. He had a number at his disposal. Annabel was one, and so he used it. He persuaded and encouraged images of her to fill his consciousness, to chase away the impossible truth that had been revealed at the flat in Moscow Road. Annabel, he remembered, smelt of vanilla pods and amber. Her skin was soft and warm. There were no sharp edges; all her curves were gentle. She was what he needed, like a soft cashmere blanket one got out of a linen cupboard on bitter winter days when blizzards blow and winds howl. He cooked lots of rice pudding at this time and poured strawberry jam all over it. Then he sat in his armchair and thought about Annabel. He longed to talk to her, to tell her everything. He thought a lot about what to give her for Christmas and where to take her for Christmas lunch. He thought about the wonder of her magnificent breasts, the colour of alabaster, her creamy nipples that tasted very slightly of nutmeg and marshmallows. These things comforted him; the thoughts and images created by his mind helped him to get through the pain, the disbelief of Judith's admission.

People didn't help. How could they? They didn't know. Who could he tell? What could he say? He did irrational things like swimming in the Serpentine. He'd been a superb swimmer since early childhood and quickly discovered the cold rush that wiped all thoughts away. There was nothing but the sensation, the tingling on his skin as he hit the water. Crash, splash, and then oblivion as he put his head underneath and swam until he thought his lungs would burst. Emerging into that first breath of air was like exploding into life. It became addictive.

Sam got a dog. He was ten months old, and his name was Bertie Basset. Bertie had long walks in Kensington Gardens on freezing winter days and waited while Sam had his swim. He was kind to this troubled man and became his confidant. They sat together by the roaring log fire in the lounge, which Sam had emptied of books, curtains, and so on after Virginia's death. A large comfortable sofa remained, and that was where they sat, night after night. Sam told Bertie everything. He was the world's best listener. He never interrupted or said the wrong thing; he just listened.

'Shall I sell this house?' Sam mused. 'Shall I sell everything and buy a house in Hampstead village, near the Heath, and we can walk every day, all day if we want. I can read and write.'

Bertie Basset had come from Richard Steel, who lived in a house near Holland Park and was about forty. He was officially Sam's solicitor, but there was more to it than that. There was a special rapport between the two men and always had been. Richard had been a young man, fresh out of law school, when he'd been given the job of wrapping up Sam's father's estate. It was a big job for a newly qualified solicitor. He was lucky, and he knew it. Richard had a mass of bright red hair and a thick beard that was not long, but curly. He was very thin and over six feet tall. He bred basset hounds and had achieved some success at Crufts. When Virginia died he'd thought of giving a dog to Sam as a gift but hadn't got round to it, for this was not to be hurried.

However, when Sam came round to change his will and remove Judith from it, it seemed clear that he needed a very special friend. Bertie was portable. He would fit comfortably into Sam's vehicle and, thus, into his busy life. Sam seemed so alone at this time. Richard didn't know what had produced his friend's dissolution. It didn't matter – it was none of his business anyway.

One evening, when they'd been discussing matters, Bertie had appeared in the doorway of Richard's study. He'd walked over to Sam and sat on him as if the matter were already settled. There was nothing to be said. As Sam got up to leave, Bertie followed him, unbidden, and plonked himself on the seat of the car. No words were spoken. They drove off together and, on arriving home, shared soup and bread. It went on from there. Soon they were inseparable. It seemed as if Bertie sensed where he was needed and where he could do most good.

Richard went to evening classes on Wednesdays. He taught employment law at one of the new colleges. Afterwards, he went to Sam's house for supper. This was something positive. Sam began to look forward to these evenings and the presence of this wild and somewhat eccentric acquaintance who invited him to look at his collection of medieval manuscripts. He came to love them and spent many evenings with Richard, drinking good wine and contemplating the beauty of these objects. It was the brilliance of the colours that drew him in initially, the way the letters wove exquisite patterns around tiny figures. This became a meditation for Sam; there was a perfection here, and also a peace. Most of all, there was harmony, and this was what Sam craved more than anything, for that is what had been lost. The world in which he moved, the sea in which he swam, had vanished, but here, in this house, he could experience tranquillity. Richard never asked difficult questions, questions that could never be answered.

'Why did you never marry, Richard?' Sam asked one evening.

'I don't consider such matters important,' he replied.

'I see,' Sam murmured, realizing immediately that this was a man with no curiosity and, therefore, no imagination; that was why he was so valuable.

'You're unusual'

'I am, but that's okay,'

'You don't ask me questions. You must be curious. Aren't you?'

'A little, but not very,' Richard said.

'I'll go now.'

'Cheerio.'

It was a bright night. The moon was full. Frost and starlight illuminated the street. Sam and Bertie turned down Bayswater Road into Pembridge Road. As they did so, Sam saw a man who he thought looked vaguely familiar outside the Sun in Splendour. The man was clearly drunk, but it was more than that. He shuffled and looked old, yet he was young. He fell, and Sam went towards him, realizing it was Claude. He hadn't seen the younger man for some weeks and was shocked at the change that had occurred. He just stared. The figure said, 'What you staring at? Why don't you just fuck off? Go on, fuck off out of it.'

'It's Sam. You remember me, don't you?'

'Yeah, I remember,' he muttered.

The two men walked slowly, arm in arm, back to Sam's house, a distance of only a few metres. Once there, Claude collapsed on to the sofa and slept.

The morning saw a heavy snowstorm. London was at a standstill; so, consequently, were Sam and Claude. News came in about other parts of the country where there had been blizzards. They were marooned in this house, at least for the time being. Sam made toast. There were at least four varieties of jam on offer that morning. All of them had something unique to offer. Oddly enough, both of them chose raspberry.

'How are you?' Sam asked eventually.

'How do you think I am?'

Silence sat between them, occupying every level. It spread like a paralysis, cutting them off from one another; yet, there was also a sharing. They poured coffee for one another. They passed the toast across the table and poured spoonfuls of jam over it.

'I suppose it's some kind of illness. I've written her a letter. She's not able to respond.'

'What did you say in the letter?' Sam murmured.

'I told her that if she couldn't tell me what was wrong, then our relationship was over. She's completely changed in the time I've known her. I know we came to know each other in a strange environment France was an idyllic location and that kind of beauty is bound to affect people. But the transformation is…unreal. Yes, that's the word. There is something about all this that's weird, sinister even. I find visiting her frightening.'

'Yes, I know. So do I,' Sam confessed.

'It's all since her mother died, isn't it? It's metamorphosis.'

'That's true.'

'Was she very close to her mother?'

'Can any child be close to an alcoholic mother?' Sam snapped.

'How long had she been alcoholic?'

'Since Harry died,' Sam replied.

'Who was…Harry?'

'Our first child, I tried to console her. I failed.'

The sky was dark. Sam left the kitchen and went into the lounge. He lit the large wood-burning stove. Slowly, and with unnecessary deliberation, he placed the paper and the sticks one on top of another. It was the basis of fire. It blazed, and the room filled with a deep orange glow, reminiscent of sunshine. For some time, he just stared at it.

Suddenly he got up, picked up his bag from the hall, and strode towards Kensington Gardens and the freezing water of the Serpentine. On arrival, he threw off most of his clothes and hurled himself into the freezing water. Pain shot around his body, but only for moments. Soon he was swimming, taking long strides, and as he did so, he felt the blood coursing through his veins as never before. Crawl, breaststroke, butterfly – it became gradually more and more exhilarating the longer he swam. He felt his heart pounding in his chest as his lungs filled with frozen air. A form of intense meditation, this freed him of every thought and every emotion. He was conscious only of his body, its motion, and its temperature. He got out, rubbed himself with his towel, put on his cosy sweater and trousers, and walked rapidly towards Westbourne Grove. He noticed that, as soon as he stopped swimming and put on his clothes, his emotions returned – the guilt, the anger, and the grief converged on his consciousness like lead. The icy water, this anaesthetic, had gone, at least for another day.

Comfort of a different sort arrived at Carluccio's. He ordered a large plate of lasagne with green salad. It arrived steaming hot and smelling of basil and tomatoes. As he ate, he felt the warmth in his stomach gradually permeating his body. The contrast with the cold of the Serpentine emphasized the heat in the food. This was the first time he'd thought with any kind of compassion since that day. What on earth would he say? What could he say? He'd never felt so lonely, so lost or so bereft as he did at this time. It was difficult to envisage any kind of future. In fact, there was no future. Judith had robbed him of his future. What would he say when people spoke to him about his daughter? What should he do about Claude? Should Claude be told the truth?

I'll ring John Antony; that's what I'll do. I'll ring him. Sam ordered a large espresso. People came and went, hugging Christmas gifts. Daughters came with their mothers. Fathers came with their daughters. Mothers and fathers came with their daughters. They drank coffee, ate cake, and then left. More daughters arrived. The world was full of mirth and daughters – all he saw were daughters. He ordered a bottle of Chianti and drank it, surrounded by families – happy, laughing families. It seemed that afternoon as if the world were full of daughters. He wished he could steal one. A grown-up one would be best or maybe a teenage one or maybe one about eight years old. Tears ran down his face.

He left the restaurant and decided to go and look for a present for Annabel. This gave him pleasure, and he chose two things. One was a beautiful laptop case made of leather and softly padded; he had a monogram put on it – 'A' for Annabel. The second present was a bottle of perfume, one that he particularly liked, but his wife had never worn it – 'Beautiful' by Estée Lauder. The lady at the counter was helpful and kind. He described Annabel to her, and the lady thought this fragrance would be nice. He smelt it and thought it desirable, both for him and her.

The assistant wrapped it up for him in silver paper and placed a gold bow on top of it.

He walked home in deep thought.

I'll tell Claude. If he's still there when I get back, I'll tell him. It's the best thing to do, the only honourable way forward, and then he can start to rebuild his life.

The snow was falling, the streets strangely silent that night, so he wandered on, looking forward to the hot fire that he knew awaited him. On arrival, he found Claude in the garden with the snow falling all over him.

'Come on in, Claude. I'll make us a pot of tea and muffins. It's the only thing for times like this.'

There was little response. It seemed from the way the snow lay that he'd been sitting there all day. Eventually, he went inside. Muffins arrived, dripping with butter and rich, heavy damson jam. The two men sat in silence, munching away as if they had known each other for centuries.

Sam thought what a lovely son-in-law he would have made if only…he could put it back together again. *Humpty Dumpty sat on a wall, Humpty Dumpty had a great fall. All the king's horses and all the king's men couldn't put Humpty together again.*

That was it, really – no one could put Humpty together again. Yet, he determined at least to try; he made a decision to trust Claude. He had to trust someone. How, he asked himself, would it be possible to retain this terrible knowledge within himself for the rest of his life? To hold on to this secret forever would be impossible. It was, he knew, possible – likely even – that he would go to the police. Nevertheless, he decided to tell Claude the truth.

'Judith killed her mother.'

A look of horror came over Claude's face as he took in the words – strange words, unbelievable words.

'I can't believe it. People don't kill their mothers. It's not something people do.'

'Believe it, believe it.'

Sam watched intently as Claude stared into the blazing fire, watching the play of orange, red, and yellow on the logs as they sparked and spat. It was not difficult to comprehend there was nothing wrong with his choice of nouns and verbs. Yet at some level these words were meaningless. Sam knew it. These words did not travel along neuronal pathways so that they could be processed and understood. The connections between brain and being snapped, it was impossible for Claude to absorb the information. He sat there by the fire and stared straight in front of him.

****

Claude felt as if he'd been confiscated, taken away. He felt nothing – not anger, nor sadness, nor hatred. Night fell, and with it came sleep. In the night, he dreamt of 9/11 – crushed bodies, detonated skyscrapers, people wandering alone and afraid through mounds of rubble looking for their loved ones but unable to recognize them from pictures, unable to find their way despite intricate detailed maps. There are no maps here. This is an unknown land, and all the ways through it have turned to dust. This was his memory, his future, his beginning and his end.

The next day, there was tea, toast, and jam on the table. Sam said he'd had a bad night, and he was going out.

'Please stay here, for a while at least. I need the company,' he said before he left.

'I want to stay, if that's okay. This isn't the time to live alone in big houses, not for either of us. We'd probably go mad right now if we were on our own for too long. It's not good, this aloneness. The weather's not right either, not for isolation. College closed for Christmas yesterday, and that's been my sanity in the last few months,' Claude replied.

Sam left as quickly as he could. He got into his car and drove once more to Kensington Gardens. He parked, got out, and walked rapidly towards the Serpentine. This time was very different; the despair had deepened overnight. He hoped the cold would kill him, swallow him up and stop his heart from beating. He hurled himself into the water and his thoughts stopped; his feelings lay suspended, frozen and inert. He swam in the icy water. He could not drown. He was too strong. It was not what he wanted. He wished that he could drown, but he was such a strong swimmer that this would be impossible without weights. He hadn't reached that point yet, but he knew he might, and that day was drawing closer.

He dried himself and threw on his warm jumper. This reminded him of his daughter. She had bought it for him one Christmas, memory took him back to that day four years ago. She got it from under the tree and passed it to him. He unwrapped it with anticipation, and this soft, red object landed at his feet.

The memory of this gift, its cosiness and warmth, drove the despair deeper and deeper. It was quickly followed by another memory – Judith when she was a tiny girl, sitting on the bed with him and looking at the wonderful illustrations in The Wind in the Willows. He recalled the day that she said she wanted to draw like that when she grew up. He'd immediately bought some paint. Her love affair with that strange medium called paint began. Sam remembered vividly his tremendous pride when she was accepted at the Royal Academy to do the four- year degree in painting and sculpture.

Where could he go from here? How could he return, how could they return to where they both were?

What is the way through this maze? he asked himself. He couldn't find any path back to normality. *What is normal? Normality is gone. Do I leave normality behind? Is that what I do?*

Yet, there was cold in winter, warm fires, and hot toast. Kensington Gardens was exactly the same as it had always been. The queen was still there. There were pavements and clear blue skies. It snowed, and the sun shone. Yet somehow it was not his sun, for this was no longer his world. Nowhere was comfortable. Life was a pair of shoes that didn't fit.

He walked until he came to the Greek Orthodox Church, where he discovered there was a service going on. He went inside and sat down in one of the pews. Glancing round, he saw the glorious icons that covered the walls. The liturgy was being sung. The priests were dressed in gold vestments. The scent of incense filled his nostrils. It was not his thinking that changed or even his feelings. It was perception.

I'm more than feelings; I'm more than my mind, more than my body. These are aspects of me, but they are not me. For surely I am more than the sum of my parts Conversely, Judith is a murderer. But she is more, much more, than that. So, what I return to is the rest of her. Sam's thoughts went round and round in this direction as he sat there in the church. The sound around him soothed him. His thoughts grew kinder, gentler.

He determined to visit John Antony before going home, so he arrived unannounced, rang the bell of the flat, and was welcomed with the promise of tea and cake.

He sat down, and the hot beverage soon arrived, accompanied by an enormous Christmas cake. John cut him a large slice and an equally large one for himself.

'How are you?'

'I can't see…anything but darkness.'

'How can…? What, if anything, can I do Help me see a way that I can put it right. How can anyone or anything put this right?'

'Some things can never be put right,' John Antony replied.

'How can there be any future after this? This is the question I ask myself every day.'

'Sam, do you…want to continue with your business, the property business I mean?'

'I can't concentrate any more. All of it was my fault. There were things I could have done, but I didn't. Why didn't I do anything? That's what I can't understand.'

'It wasn't all your fault. It wasn't your fault that Harry died, and that was the trigger for her addiction.'

'I should have done something,'

'What do you mean?'

'There were things… I could have done more.'

'Do you think there's anything that you could do now?'

'I want to make amends, but it's too late. The damage is done.'

'There are things you could do to help people in the future,'

'Philanthropy, is that what you mean?'

'If that's what you want to call it,'

'I worked; she drank. That was the way it was. In the middle was Judith.'

He walked home, lost in thought, and picked up the post, which had lain undisturbed all day. It was mostly Christmas cards, but there was, at the bottom, a mail-order catalogue, which his wife liked particularly. He went into the kitchen and put the kettle on. Toast went into the toaster, and honey emerged from the cupboard. He opened the catalogue as he drank the scalding tea. It revealed pages of warm, elegant sweaters. He glanced at them all, wondering about the virtues of each one. Then there was the stab of memory. Last winter, he and his wife had found a present for Judith here. Immediately, he let the catalogue fall to the floor. He picked it up and saw that it had fallen open on a page revealing a sumptuous velvet dressing gown. He stared at the midnight blue colour and the way it fell in generous folds around the model who looked not unlike his own daughter. Sam picked up the phone, dialled the number, and ordered one to be sent immediately to his daughter's address.

It was about that time that he began to watch her flat. He watched from his car for hours, just waiting for her to emerge. Some part of him wanted to approach her, but what would he say? He wanted to stay where everything was warm, he could control his thoughts and, ultimately, the ideas that emerged from them. If he went to her, control would be lost. Feelings might escape, feelings that he couldn't deal with or understand. What did he feel? He didn't know how he felt, and because he didn't know, he was afraid. He did not have that knowledge, that certainty in the abidingness of love; and, because he did not have it, he was afraid.

One day, about a week before Christmas, there was a lot of activity around Judith's flat. A van with the name of a famous art gallery drew up outside. Four men went inside and stayed for a couple of hours. Eventually, they emerged with what looked like a huge canvas covered with layers of cloth, which could have been velour, velvet, or wool. They placed the canvas in the van. Judith herself emerged, dressed in her long black velvet coat. On her head she had a thick woollen beret. Her face, as before, had that gothic quality; the alabaster skin looked like polished marble. Sam noticed that her hair had grown a little since they'd last met in November. There was a whisper of a curl beneath the beret. It seemed as if she was being taken off somewhere – not against her will, but transported somewhere nevertheless. In another place and in another time it could have been Siberia. *I would so hate it if she were going to Siberia. I do care about where she is going. I do care. I do mind.*

He followed the van through the streets of London, until it reached Knightsbridge. It stopped outside a world-famous art gallery. Four men got out carrying the cloth-covered canvas. They took it gently up the steps and into the gallery. The door closed behind them. These men were inside with his only daughter, and he was outside, and he couldn't see, or hear, or know anything. What Sam did know at that time was that he desperately wanted to be where those four men were, with his daughter. It was late and dark when she emerged. It was also snowing and bitterly cold. Judith walked briskly along the pavement. Suddenly, Sam left his car and ran towards her, enclosing her in his arms. Thoughts of the day she was born flooded his mind. He looked into her face and thought of her suffering, the suffering that had, in the end, become unendurable. The need to put it right engulfed him.

She left him without a backward glance and hurried home as fast as she could go.

****

Claude wandered around in Sam's garden, lit by the street light. He walked round and round, conscious only of the crunch beneath his feet and the frozen air against his face. He didn't leave. He dreaded home and work and everything connected to life and living. The next moment, he felt annoyed with himself. *After all,* he reasoned, *I haven't known her long.* Why do I feel like this? Sam's living room was warm and cosy. It seemed to matter less to him that it was not home. He needed to be here in this place – not at the college, not at home, but here.

Where do I want to be now? Possibly in monastery, somewhere where I can just paint and think and be. No, that's not it. What I want now is Paris, the Rue d'Orléans. I'll go walking in Paris. That's what I'll do. It is, after all, the most beautiful walk in the world. I'll let the house and go to Paris for a year. I can paint and wander at will. The idea entered his mind and held him in confusion and amazement. What did he want? Why this idea, at this time, and in this place? Maybe he could find peace there and tranquillity – most of all, he would find himself. He would let his house and just paint, wander in and out of cafes, and visit the bars where Hemingway and

Sartre drank, thought, and wrote. It would be healing to absorb new things and new places, just to go and think and be. This warm house was bringing clarity and silence. He would wander in Paris; stay in the Rue de l'Odéon or the Rue d'Orléans; mingle with artists, writers, and painters; drink coffee and cognac; and paint to his heart's content.

CHAPTER SEVENTEEN

In Geoffrey's department in Handford, all hell had broken loose. The next few weeks would be very busy indeed. One Tuesday, the phone had gone in the middle of the night. He'd woken up abruptly. It was the night sister on the addiction unit.

'Hello, Dr Dove, I'm sorry to wake you, but I don't know what to do.'

'What's the matter?' he replied sharply. He hated being wakened. 'Can't the duty registrar deal with all this? I'll be in in the morning, first thing.'

'Dr Crowther wants to admit Mr Reynolds. I told him you insisted that he was one of the clients we were not to readmit because he's been in here six times. We're not getting anywhere.'

'Put Dr Crowther on to me,'

'Hello, Dr Dove. I think we have no option but to readmit. The daughter's been on the phone pleading with me to admit her father. She said he's hitting her mother,'

'No, we are not going to readmit. Tell the daughter to ring the police, tell them how violent he is, and get them over there at once,' Geoffrey replied impatiently.

'You're making a mistake. You haven't spoken to the daughter,'

'Do as I tell you. Do not readmit!' Geoffrey shouted down the phone. Why was Dr Crowther so...so determined? Quite simply, he had no responsibility for the budget, just for the patients in his care. At times, he appeared unable to appreciate the larger picture.

Geoffrey looked at the clock. It was 5 a.m. He knew he wouldn't sleep. He couldn't sleep; this is how it was every night. He had a bloody cold. He tried to read but couldn't concentrate, so he went downstairs, put on the kettle and made coffee. He popped two pieces of toast into the toaster. When it was ready, he smothered it with plum jam.

Ferney House always had a surfeit of these wondrous fruit conserves. As he munched away at his toast, his mood changed. He was calmer, clearer. He thought about Mrs Reynolds and how hard this woman had tried to keep the family together. He'd gotten to know her well over the last five years and liked her very much. But it was more than that – he respected her. He thought of her life with her husband and wondered how she would emerge this time. She was fiercely intelligent, and there was steel in her veins when it came to survival and defending this man against the worst horrors of his illness. She rescued him again and again from the nightmares he created for himself – unemployment, epilepsy, gastritis. There was so much that was ghastly in her life. He'd tried to make matters easier. She'd come to trust him; he was a shoulder for her to lean on in the worst times, for example when her husband's delirium tremens were torturing him while he attempted alcohol withdrawal. Usually, he imagined his face being devoured by rats, and then the screaming would start, the begging for alcohol, the head-battering, the banging, the running away as he attempted to escape from his darkest fear.

Geoffrey thought of the times when he'd controlled the worst of Mr Reynolds' delusions with various drugs and then the conversations that would go on for days, weeks even, and progress was made.

It never lasted. He could not sustain it. David couldn't maintain sobriety for more than a month. It was often less than that. One house would be repossessed and then another, and so it went on. The rent would remain unpaid, and the family would move again and again.

But with the support of his unit, they had managed to stay together in Handford, and there had been a place of safety, a refuge where some trace of normality could be found.

It was a nightmare existence for Mrs Reynolds and her children. They never tried to make friends with people – the isolation was easier to cope with. Mrs Reynolds told him that sometimes her husband could be persuaded to go to AA meetings but not often, and it didn't seem to work anyway. He came home grumpy and miserable. He told her the spectacle of drunks getting up and telling their stories repulsed him. He didn't go for the idea of the 'higher power'. The children would always try to protect their mother against David's drunken aggression. At the family sessions, which Geoffrey held monthly on the unit, they would describe the fear they felt, saying they never knew what to do or how to deal with it. Once, in a particularly harrowing session, one of David's children said he wished his father were dead. Geoffrey suspected that many children felt like that, but few, if any, had the courage to say it. This was the destructive nature of alcohol addiction. It permeated the soul, not just of the alcoholics, but of those who had the misfortune to love them.

How brave, how brave these children are, he thought. They knew that their mother provided food, safety, and love, so all they wanted was to preserve her intact, no matter what. She was their saviour, and in their own strange way, they were hers. These thoughts and memories floated through his mind as he ate his toast, had his shower, and got dressed.

Geoffrey got into his car and drove to the hospital. He put Amy Winehouse on his stereo. Her voice soothed him; his thoughts softened, rising smoothly without malice.

It was 9 a.m. when he at last arrived at the unit. He walked along the corridor to his consulting room. His secretary spoke in a hushed voice when she brought in the coffee.

'Dr Crowther asked me to give you this as soon as you arrived,' she said.

Geoffrey opened the envelope and read:

> Just to keep you updated – Mrs Reynolds is in intensive care, Mr Reynolds has been arrested, social services have taken the children to an emergency foster home.
>
> C. Crowther

'Have I appointments now? When?' he enquired after reading and rereading the message. The enormity of what had happened took time to assimilate.

'Not until eleven thirty, this afternoon, you have a meeting with Miss Griffiths,' she replied.

Geoffrey strode out of his unit, crossed the hospital car park, and entered the hospital. He leapt up the stairs to the ITU and rang the bell. Showing his identity, he asked to see Mrs Reynolds. The doctor, who knew Geoffrey, was reluctant at first to divulge what had happened. At last, he explained that she had been admitted at 7 a.m. with severe head injuries and that her neck had been broken just above her collarbone.

Geoffrey looked at this woman. The huge facial contusions would have made her unrecognizable had he not been guided to her bed. He felt his heart beating, his breathing increasing. Rage engulfed him.

'How was her neck broken?' he muttered.

'I'm not sure whether it was the blow to the right or left of the head that caused the neck to snap. She has haemorrhages in both hemispheres, so it's difficult to know exactly which blow snapped the neck.'

'Is she going to…be…live, I mean?'

'If she does survive, she'll be paralysed from the neck down.'

'Theatre?'

'She will go to theatre within the hour.'

Geoffrey felt something akin to fear, but it was something else entirely.

It was about himself. Why, he wondered, could he not merely detach himself from what was going on and distance himself from the entire procedure, from what had happened? Why did he feel so responsible?

He didn't know exactly why he felt so ghastly about this particular case. He knew perfectly well that there are some people you simply cannot help. For whatever morbid, genetic, or chemical reason, they are simply not susceptible to treatment. Why couldn't he just accept that he'd done all that he could do for Mr Reynolds? The health service had done all it could be expected to do, and yet…there remained a sense of futility and failure. If he couldn't make a difference in the life of that family, then what, he wondered, did his own life amount to?

What exactly am I for? he asked. What is the taxpayer paying me for? It is paying me to support the vulnerable and the weak. Surely that is what I am for. Isn't it?

****

Annabel arrived at the doctor's surgery about five minutes early. The waiting room was packed with people coughing and spluttering and children behaving like wild animals. When her turn at last arrived, she sat down in the surgery. The doctor looked at the computer screen, at her, and back again.

'Ah, yes, the blood tests have come back, as well as the urine tests. You are perfectly healthy. The sickness and nausea are symptoms of your pregnancy. You're six weeks pregnant, or thereabouts. It seems the baby was conceived some time in late October.'

'Are you sure?' Her thoughts went into overdrive, working things out – dates, events, feelings. That was when Geoffrey went to Switzerland and she went to London and slept with Sam. She flipped quickly through the pages of her diary, and there it was; in the middle of October, she went to London and stayed with Ruth for ten days. Geoffrey was at the conference in Switzerland. The only man she had slept with was Sam, and it had definitely been in October. The shock of this realization numbed her mind. She sat in the surgery staring into space. She asked once again if it was certain.

'Yes, there's no doubt about it. You will need to go for a scan. But, as I said, it would have been some time in October. I'll make an appointment for you.'

'How long will I have to wait?'

'About two weeks I should imagine. But it's Christmas, and that always complicates matters.'

'I need to know before Christmas during my break.'

'I see.'

Well, you could go privately and it would be done in the next few days at the Nuffield. I'll ring them now if you like and see when they could fit you in.'

'Yes, please do that.'

The answer was quick. They could fit her in that afternoon at 2.pm.

'Thank God for that. I'll go. October was confusing, bewildering… I need to know where I stand. There'll be decisions to be made.'

''Of course, if you need anything, you know where I am.'

'Thank you, you've been kind and helpful.'

She got up and left, got into her car, and drove home. On arrival, she rummaged in her drawer for her diary and dates. She double-checked everything on her computer, as well as in her handwritten diary, which she kept beside her bed. No – there was no doubt about it. The doctor had said that the baby was probably conceived in October. The child was Sam's. This realization brought a strange, unexpected joy to Annabel's heart. She felt happy as she went to the Nuffield for her scan and even happier when they gave her the results and a picture of the tiny creature inside her womb.

So, this, she thought, is life. This is where it all begins, inside our mother's womb. This is the place where we hear the first sounds of life, where we first move. This is the place that provokes our first idea, our first thought, our first feeling – and this life began that day in late October with Sam.

Oh, how she longed to ring him, but she hesitated, and then she felt frightened and alone. She arrived at the Nuffield at 2 p.m. and went straight in. The nurse was very pleasant indeed, which was so important for Annabel at this time. The thick gel placed on her stomach was as cold as the weather outside, but the sound of the scanner soothed her, and she saw, as if among a fog, a little blob of life.

'Look. Look. Can you see?' the nurse said excitedly.

At first, Annabel shook her head. But the nurse directed her gaze. And there it was – a tiny little collection of cells, her cells and Sam's joined together. She cried. The nurse comforted her and brought her a hot cup of tea and a digestive biscuit. Annabel looked at her and thought how lovely she was.

She got into her car and sorted through her CDs. *What is the perfect sound for this moment in my life?* she wondered. Something gentle. She decided eventually on Leonard Cohen simply for the husky sound of his voice and the gentle poetry. 'Suzanne' blared out from the speakers as she drove towards the hospital; her thoughts settled into silent reverie.

At four o'clock that afternoon, she was scheduled to meet Geoffrey to assess how things were going in the addiction unit.

'I've thought a lot about what you said about the addiction unit since we last spoke,' she said as soon as he walked into her office.

'Yes.'

'What, if anything, do you know about Mrs Reynolds?'

'Mrs Reynolds, who on earth is Mrs Reynolds?' she replied.

'Mrs Reynolds is in ITU with a broken neck. Her husband beat her until she was – is – unrecognizable. He's been a patient of mine for years. I've gotten to know her and her children very well,' Geoffrey said while staring out of the window on to the car park below.

Annabel looked at him and then at the floor. She played with a pen on her desk, picking it up, putting it down again. 'I'm sorry. I'm so sorry, Geoffrey. I'll recommend to the trust that your specialized addiction unit is spared as much as possible.'

'It's a little late! Just a little. What, I ask you, what is a hospital for? What am I for?' he said shaking with rage.

'I'm not responsible. I'm not a moral philosopher; nor am I a social worker,' Annabel replied with the kind of cold logic that led people, especially work colleagues, to dislike her.

'No, but you are a bloody human being. There is, Annabel, more than one way to kill someone. You don't always need a knife or a gun or even a noose. Indifference will do nicely. How neatly and cleanly the callous kill.'

'I was employed to do a specific job, to advise the hospital trust on possible ways to reduce this huge deficit. I'm being paid to do this job, and I will do it to the very best of my ability. There is no other way for me,' she said.

'What good is anyone or anything without compassion? What use are you or I?'

He left the office without warning and without a backward glance. Suddenly, she wanted out. This meeting had served to remove all doubt from her mind. It had cleansed her and made her realize that sorting out deficits for inefficient healthcare trusts was not what she wanted to do with her life. She could, and would, take her career in another direction altogether.

Why, she thought as she sat there in that office, should I be lumbered, burdened with guilt? How dare he do that to me? What am I supposed to feel about the Reynolds family? Now all this bloody business about compassion.

She was, she knew, both kind and compassionate. She knew that about herself; her relationship with Claude had taught her that much, if nothing else. Annabel decided there and then that she never wanted to see Geoffrey again. Mrs Bloody Reynolds could have left this monster of a man if she'd wanted to. Why did she stay with him? She had a responsibility for her own life. Don't we all have that? Why did she stay when she could have gone? Didn't she consider what was best for her children? These questions and more hurtled through her mind at terrifying speed, tipping it into overdrive.

There was no way she could concentrate on the deficits. She ran downstairs to her car and drove into the centre of town. She went to Starbucks and ordered a grande latte and then she had another with caramel syrup. While Annabel sat there in that cafe, on that day, at that time…Mrs Reynolds died.

Annabel kept reading and rereading the text that arrived on her mobile: 'Mrs Reynolds is dead. Geoffrey.'

It was then, in that coffee shop, that it first began – the haunting. She did not know then that she would think about Mrs Reynolds at least once every day for the rest of her life. Slowly, she walked out into the street and back to her car. A lone tear ran down her face as she drove. She didn't wipe it away but let it linger there as a mark of respect.

The phone rang as Annabel returned to her flat. She picked it up. It was her sister.

'Hello, it's me, Ruth. I haven't heard from you for ages and ages. I wondered if you were all right.'

There was a silence. Annabel didn't know how to reply. Eventually, she said, 'I'm many things at the moment; all right isn't one of them.'

'Are you coming up for Christmas?'

'Yes, on the twenty-third of December.'

'Not until then?'

'No I finish work on the twenty-second.'

'I see. Well, I can't argue with that.'

'No,' Annabel murmured.

'Are you okay?'

'I'm many things. Okay isn't one of them. I just told you.'

'I'll come down, shall I?'

'Just leave me be,' she replied at last.

The run-up to the week's meeting with the trust managers and the auditors was hectic. Annabel lived on her nerves and her extraordinary mental energy. On the first day, she produced the budget of each department and, the following day, the five-year projections. The rest of the week was spent discussing the various options she had proposed. There was argument and counterargument, some of it heated and some less so. There were periods of rational debate and periods of passionate discord, where no one could agree on the best way forward. Somewhere at the back of Annabel's mind, no matter how hard she pushed her away, sat Mrs Reynolds.

What is it? Annabel asked herself. *Why does she so often fill my mind when I least expect it?* She had no idea of the answer, no idea at all. She did know that she felt disturbed; uncomfortable; and very, very unhappy.

Home she went to TV dinners, soaps, hot baths, and bed. The extraordinary thing about Annabel was that she had the capacity to put Mrs Reynolds at the back of her mind, to place her in a pigeonhole inside her brain until her work was done. Work was paramount. Getting a result, working through options – these were her priorities and her strengths.

The following day was press day. The vultures were coming in the afternoon, so she had to concentrate on her appearance. The press conference was, as always, a strain. It wasn't the questions, for she always knew the answers; they could not faze her, no matter how hard they tried. However, the death of Mrs Reynolds had turned them into vultures, and they were out for blood. This story would sell newspapers – they would fly off the shelves, and the vultures knew it. A hospital had not admitted Mr Reynolds, despite the pleas of his daughter and his wife had died of the most horrific injuries. These were the facts, and there was no way they could be disputed. The chairman of the trust appeared and tried to quieten the hysteria. He said that difficult choices had been made and would continue to be made. He expressed deep regret and sympathy for the family but went on to say that the hospital had supported the Reynolds family for over five years and that Mr Reynolds had been admitted into the treatment programme six times without success.

The trust managers were again attacked when they announced the decision to reduce ITU beds by one and to reduce the money spent on psychiatric services. This was, they explained, the only way that the provision of expensive drugs for both cancer and Alzheimer's could be sustained in the face of the deficit. It was a clear choice, and they had made it. The greatest happiness for the greatest number – this was the guiding principle by which they had made the decisions they had made.

The day ended with Annabel realizing that the bulk of her job was done. Decisions had been made. At last, she could go to London and relax – except for Mrs Reynolds, who was to remain forever in the hidden recesses of her mind.

CHAPTER EIGHTEEN

The next day dawned. It was a dark, damp December morning. There was something about the darkness and there was something about the warm enclosed space that was her motor car. She was going home for Christmas. She loaded her car and left the dank and dreary city far behind. She drove to London and eventually arrived at her sister's house, by which time the sun had broken through.

'God, it's so good to see you. It seems as if you've been in Handford forever.'

'I think I have. Was there life before I went there?'

'Robin's staying in New York, with his woman. So it's just you and me, I'm afraid. The house isn't full of children, as it usually is.'

'I'm sorry, Ruth. I've not been here for you, have I?'

'You've been you; that's all. There've been times when I wished I hadn't persuaded you to go to Handford, but it was the right thing, wasn't it?'

'What's right, what's wrong? I don't know any more. I don't know anything any more.'

'Let's have some tea. I've made a lovely Christmas cake. I think it's one of my best,' Ruth replied.

'When did Robin leave?'

'Physically, he left two months ago, but in every other way he left long before that.'

'Tell me.'

'There's nothing to say. I'm okay about it, pleased in fact. He's been generous. I'm to have the freehold of the house. Love dies sometimes, Annabel. There's no point hanging on when something is over.'

Ruth had always been strong, stoic even. She allowed things to move in the way they wanted to. It was a characteristic that nurtured people and drew others towards her.

'We'd reached the end of the road. If you try to hang on, it just builds resentment and hatred in the end. Who wants that?' she went on.

'I admire you,' Annabel whispered.

'And I you, shall we sit here eating, drinking, laughing, and crying all over Christmas?'

'Yes, it's perfect.'

'What about you?'

'I can't even begin. It would take a lifetime. Just pretend not to be cross. Is that a deal?'

'Well, that's a tall order.'

'Just tell me,' Ruth murmured.

'Tomorrow, after I've slept. Otherwise, it'll be unintelligible.'

She went upstairs and found her bedroom full of flowers. She ran a hot bath and stretched out in the warm water, and then she got into bed and slept until morning.

****

It arrived, as mornings always do. The high streets were full of people. There were Christmas trees everywhere hanging with baubles. There was laughter. There was company. Annabel and Ruth spent the whole day in the shops, their arms crammed full of parcels of every size and dimension. They returned home about six o'clock and sat by the fire, wrapping presents. Annabel's mobile rang. She saw it was Sam.

'Why don't you pick up?' asked Ruth.

Annabel didn't answer it. She kept sipping mulled wine and

wrapping her presents without replying to her sister. The next day was Christmas Eve, and she'd said nothing about the events of the previous months. Ruth went to bed.

It was not shaping up well, this Christmas – cold, dark and friendless. This was not what either had planned. The Christmas spirit somehow wasn't there. Mrs Reynolds, whose name kept popping up, had stolen it. She wouldn't be denied access to Annabel's mind. There she lived, among the neural pathways that constitute the human brain. She would not be moved in or out of her chosen spot.

How, Annabel wondered, are those poor children, the first Christmas without their mother?

In the afternoon, Sam phoned, and this time Annabel picked up.

'Hello.'

'Dinner – how does that strike you?' he asked.

'Yes,' Annabel said, 'That would be good.'

'I'll pick you up at eight.'

'Thank you.'

'What's the address?'

'Twenty-nine Ossington Street,' she replied, as butterflies in the pit of her stomach warned of what lay ahead.

She spent much of the afternoon lying in the bath stroking her stomach and trying to take in the implications of pregnancy, of telling Sam. What then? She hardly knew him, but it was his reaction that Annabel thought most about. Motherhood – what would it be like? What does being a mother mean? She thought about her own mother. Ruth, in a sense, was her mother, and she was Ruth's. It had to be that way; it was the way it had fallen. Their mother had gone off with a strange man, their father, and the two of them now lived on some remote Scottish island, in a tumbledown cottage with few links to the mainland. She remembered the bleakness, the loneliness of their childhood. Once she and Ruth had escaped, they hadn't missed anything about it at all. There was a silent agreement between them; they would look after each other.

Annabel gazed down into the bathwater, and then she found some of her sister's bath oil and poured it in, noticing the name on the label

– Korres, made in Greece. How strange, she mused, to be content – as her mother was – with birdsong, sea sounds, and peat to make fires. There were always books. Her parents read a lot to themselves and to her when she was small. Her father was usually to be found working at his desk, translating Russian. It was how he earned his living, such as it was. These thoughts gave way to ones of Sam, in the way thoughts do. They excited her, and they caused her heart to beat that much faster than normal, even as she stretched out in the warmth of the water.

It was as if her parents were creatures who had emerged from the Stone Age, she thought. She'd grown up with the wind against her face, but it had not hardened her. Sitting on the cliffs with her mother for hours on end in silence, listening to the sea crashing against rocks until it grew dark, and then returning to the cottage to eat and then go to bed – this twilight world of solitude, the dreamlike questions about God and the world in general, answered by her mother's dreamlike answers, had conferred on her a mysteriously confused atmosphere throughout her childhood. The time she loved best was at school on the mainland. She was clever and successful.

There in the bath that afternoon, she remembered it all clearly without affection or bitterness. It was the way it was. She'd never been beaten or abused, and her mother and father loved her very much. It was just unusual. No one she knew had had a childhood of this nature. Her father jarred in Annabel's mind. He'd suffered from depression for many years. She felt a deep sadness and guilt that she'd not helped him more, that she hadn't cared about him more, that she'd devoted all her energy to her studies so that she could get to university and escape from the bleak Hebridean world.

Eventually, after about an hour, Annabel washed off her hair mask, dried herself, and wandered downstairs, where she discovered Ruth stuffing the turkey. They made hot coffee and sat down to talk by the warm fire. Sparkling presents lay around them everywhere.

'I'm going out this evening,' Annabel said, with thinly disguised enthusiasm.

'You still haven't told me anything.'

'I know.'

Slowly Annabel revealed the events of the past months. Ruth sat there and listened. She didn't interrupt. She didn't judge. She just listened, and that was, of course, her great strength.

'I just don't love Geoffrey. It's impossible to separate him from Ferney House. You can't marry someone because you love his home, the place where he lives. It's just wrong. You must see that.'

'I do, of course I do. It just seemed so perfect, and you'd been miserable for so long with Claude,' Ruth replied.

'It was all too perfect. Geoffrey was just too perfect. I don't do perfect. I do mess – it's a challenge. I love challenges. Living in the Hebrides with Mum and Dad was a bloody challenge. Even getting to school was a challenge. I hated it more than you, I'm sure.'

'Yes, you loathed it. I just disliked it, the cold and the isolation. It was a life lived in shadows.'

'Thank God we inherited that bit of money from Granny and Grandad, so we could escape.'

'Weren't they weird, Mum and Dad?'

'Crazy. They were always talking about themselves. They wanted so little. Their lives were made up almost entirely of moods and thoughts.'

'Never mind all that. What's happening tonight?'

'I'm going out with a man I met last time I was up here.'

'Where the hell did you meet him?' exclaimed Ruth.

'Carluccio's,' Annabel replied with a mischievous glint in her eye.

'Carluccio's! Not really?'

'Yes, but that's just the tip of a very large iceberg.' Annabel couldn't control her mirth. Suddenly she laughed, realizing how outrageous the whole thing was.

'You're enjoying this, aren't you?'

'What I'm going to tell you is pretty shocking, so brace yourself.' At this point Ruth threw more coal on the fire and settled herself on her beanbag. 'I'm ready now to hear the rest of the story.'

'Draw the curtains.'

In the late afternoon on Christmas Eve, Annabel told her story.

'I can hardly take in what you're saying. How little I know you,' remarked her sister at last.

'So he picked you up in Carluccio's, took you back to his place...'

Annabel froze. Memories of that night filled her mind. She thought of Sam's power, the strength that had manifested itself within and around her. How she wanted that again and again. Somehow, she knew a truth that she had not acknowledged before. This man had awoken something within her, some part of her being that no one had ever touched, some primal knowledge. The primitive pre-human part of her had emerged; all that had gone before seemed small, insignificant, and irrelevant.

The doorbell shattered the silence. Annabel left her sister without a backward glance.

She opened the door. The embrace was immediate, strong, and real, but there were no words, for there are times when they just don't work. There is some place beyond the heart, beyond love, which is known only to the few, and that place is not found or discovered through words.

The language of the body is not confined to sentences, to correct grammar, to the use of syntax – for these are tools for the civilized, the clean, and the beautiful. Annabel knew that as much as she knew anything.

****

He'd chosen a small intimate restaurant. Annabel always wore her grey velvet jacket if she was unsure of where she was going. It was a remarkable jacket, at home in the dressiest venue yet bohemian enough to flow through any lesser event. How pleased she felt that she'd thrown it over her shoulders that evening on the way out. It suited her colouring perfectly, being silver-grey. She'd bought it a long time ago from a shop specializing in 1930s vintage clothes.

They were led to a table in a small alcove illuminated by soft golden lamps. The menu arrived, and they both decided on traditional Christmas fare based on goose.

The silence persisted longer than is normal, probably because neither of them knew what to say. There was awkwardness, almost akin to fear.

They both chose consommé to start.

'It's lovely,' murmured Annabel.

The goose arrived draped in soft, warm gravy.

'You've been so busy since we last met,' Sam said at last.

'Yes, I'm a bit of a workaholic, I'm afraid.'

'Did you manage to reduce deficits?'

'Not entirely, but I managed to clarify choices, and then others made the choices for me – the hospital trust, to be precise. Have you been busy?'

'It depends what you mean by busy. It seems as if…I'm exhausted.'

'Go on.'

'My wife died in the summer.'

'Were you close?'

'No, not in the end. We married when we were very young. We were only twenty.'

'Do you want to talk about it?'

Sam didn't answer for several minutes. He felt confused, disorientated. What shall I say? he wondered. Yet a part of him longed to confide in this woman, to tell her everything.

'Why spoil a Christmas Eve? It's supposed to be jolly, isn't it?'

'Maybe happiness isn't on the agenda at the moment.'

'Not for you either?' he enquired.

'Well, it's been cold.'

'The coldness of this winter has helped me through.'

'How?' she enquired.

'In lots of ways, cold can anaesthetize. It places the mind in hibernation.

The white world has its own silence and its own peace,' he replied, looking at Annabel.

'There's been so much snow,'

'Yes. I've swum in the Serpentine every day,'

'Why on earth did you do that?'

His thoughts drifted. He took a large swig of wine before he replied.

'It made me numb. It took away emotion, memory, guilt – everything.

All I felt was ice. Ice ran through my veins, down my spine, everywhere,'

Annabel listened, for this man had the most musical voice. She just wanted the sound and the story he was telling to go on and on. 'Go on with what you were saying,'

'What about you? Tell me why you were so sad in Carluccio's. What made you cry?'

'I'll tell you but not now. Your story is what I want to hear,' she replied. 'When my wife died, it was all very sudden, like a psychological tsunami; we were thrown around by huge waves – were drowning, I suppose.'

'Are you still drowning?'

'I drowned a long time ago,' he murmured. 'Did you ever love her, I mean really love her?'

'We were very young. She excited me in strange indescribable ways, ways that I wouldn't share with anyone – certainly not with a woman I hardly know.'

'Am I a stranger?' she murmured.

'Almost,'

Annabel thought about the child she was carrying and the fact that the father thought her a stranger.

'It's almost unbelievable. There is a part of my being that doesn't believe it and probably never will,' he said at last.

'What is it, exactly?'

'The response,' he muttered.

'I see.' Annabel felt this was getting stranger by the minute.

'My response to my daughter's suffering. I could have saved her, but I didn't. I ignored it, the horror of the alcoholic mother. There is nothing so depraved, so hideous for a child than to watch its own mother sink into this dark oblivion. The place is so dark that there is no light bright enough to penetrate it.'

Annabel thought of the Reynolds family. The two stories met somewhere in the caverns of her mind, where they intermingled and danced around inside her head.

'It was alcohol that killed my wife.'

'Is your daughter dead, then?'

'Why on earth did you say that?'

Annabel looked at Sam as the confusion in her mind spread around her whole being. Why did I say that? she wondered.

He ordered a brandy for both of them. They sat in silence, watching the people arrive and then suddenly depart.

'I shouldn't have done this, spoken like this on Christmas Eve. It's the first Christmas since…Virginia died. You're so easy to talk to.'

'Don't apologize please,'

The pause made Annabel feel more vulnerable. She found herself watching her own thoughts, as if from a gallery.

'When I first met Virginia, she was dressed in brilliant yellow; it flowed around and about her like a cloud. That, is what I loved,' Sam whispered.

'How do any of us know exactly what it is we love? What is it that we love about anyone or anything?'

'Love is about so many things that we can't understand,' Sam replied.

'Or appreciate. "Who can explain it? Who can tell you why? Fools give you reasons, but wise men never try,"' she murmured.

'What has happened to my daughter is my fault entirely. I let her down. There was so much going on in my life. I don't believe I really cared about her. I tell myself I did, but it's not honest,' Sam replied.

'Perhaps that's part of the reason you swam in ice – a method of punishment. Don't you think?'

'Self-punishment – is that what you mean?'

'Well, yes. Yes, I do.'

'Families suddenly creep up on you. They wind themselves around your torso like ivy,' Sam replied.

'They're frightening, you're caught in a web.'

'Exactly. I felt devoured by her alcoholism. It was as if I were being eaten – psychologically,'

'Why didn't you leave, take your daughter and go?' Annabel asked. 'Why do you want to know?'

'I need to understand,' the confusion took hold of her mind and twisted it, shaped it like molten metal.

'Don't you think I've asked myself that question a thousand times? I believe it's about power and guilt.'

A potent combination,'

'Yes, possibly the most potent combination of all,' he whispered. Suddenly, Sam wanted to visit his daughter. He asked Annabel if she would go with him. Her curiosity had been aroused by the whole story. Maybe it was fascination or curiosity that persuaded her to go. She was not sure, but nothing could have prevented her. He paid hastily, and they hurriedly left the restaurant. They drove swiftly through the London streets that looked as though they were covered with diamonds as the moon lit up the pavements. Annabel felt shrouded in mystery. All around her, everywhere, there was nothing but mystery.

They arrived at Judith's flat to find the whole place in darkness. She was sitting alone in the living room. Annabel thought she looked like a statue that could crack at any time. She sensed a terrifying fragility in this place.

'I came because it's Christmas Eve. I had to see you.'

'Why?' Judith replied.

'I want to go home. I don't want to stay here,' Annabel felt terribly

frightened. She left, walking out into the frozen air, gasping for breath. She heard Sam calling but took no notice and walked on as fast as she could. It was about a mile from Judith's flat back to her sister's house in Westbourne Grove A few drunks wandered the streets, along with the effervescent air of parties ending and people going home.

She walked, and as she walked, she wondered how she could have fallen into this. She had been stupid, and now she was trapped. Or was she? *What am I to do? she thought. I could…get rid of the baby and return to my job in Handford. On the other hand, I could stay here in this hideous mess and try and make it better.*

The point is, you can never make it better. You can never make anything better, ever. If Claude had taught her anything, it was that. Unwillingly, her mind drifted back to Mrs Reynolds. Perhaps she had felt powerless to leave that violent husband of hers.

The seed of guilt she'd felt since her last encounter with Geoffrey sprouted more shoots that evening. They rooted themselves deep within her being, where they would stay for the rest of her life.

She put the key in the lock and turned it.

Oh God, she thought, thank God I'm here. Thank God for Ruth.

'Is that you, Annabel?' she heard her sister shout.

'Yes, it's me. Let me go to bed.'

'What on earth has happened?'

'I've been so stupid.'

Ruth tried to comfort her sister. Annabel pushed her roughly away.

'This mess is my entire fault, do you hear? It's all my fault. I'm going to completely wreck your Christmas.'

Annabel ran upstairs to the comfort of her bed, leaving Ruth dazed and lost, surrounded by lonely, glittering presents.

The night brought dreams to Annabel. Hidden somewhere was a message, a message from her unconscious. She saw, as she slept, birds flying above her and around her. They circled round and round, and then gently, they settled on the edges of the cliff, where she was hanging, clinging to the cliff, afraid to jump or to move in any direction. She lost her footing and plunged into the fast-flowing river. She let it take her wherever it wanted.

When she first woke, she thought about the dream she'd had, and then she dozed off once more. Her ideas mingled, changed direction, and blended together, rather as water does as it flows towards the sea.

It was late morning before she dragged herself out of bed.

'I haven't opened any of my presents. I've been waiting for you,' Ruth murmured.

'We could open them now.'

Ruth agreed, so they went into the lounge and found gold, silver, and red paper parcels strewn all over the floor.

Ruth opened the tiny parcel her sister handed to her. The satin-lined box contained the Raymond Weil watch Annabel had chosen for her.

'It's exquisite,' Ruth whispered.

They examined it in detail. Annabel put it on her sister's wrist. It suited her perfectly.

'Thank you, thank you so much.'

Ruth picked up the present she'd bought for Annabel, one – in fact – of several.

Annabel opened it, and inside was a deep green sweater that would keep anyone warm on the coldest of days.

The next present was soft and very large. It had so much wrapping around it that Annabel thought it would never reveal its contents. Inside was a rug that could be described as a rug of many colours. Joseph's technicolour coat came into her mind.

'Oh, it's wonderful!' she exclaimed, placing it on the floor in front of her.

'I thought it would cheer up your dreary flat in Handford,'

'It'll certainly do that.' Annabel was thrilled. This was just what she needed. It would lift her spirits whenever she came home. The card said, 'From Ruth, Mum, and Dad, with all our love.' Annabel felt ashamed. She'd done what she'd always done and found a present for her mother in a mail-order catalogue. She'd forgotten what it was. She'd just sent it by mail order. There was no thought behind any of it.

'Mum phoned this morning and said she loved the throw you sent. She asked how you were. I said you were okay, but I don't really know if that's true. Is it?'

'Somehow I don't think so.'

Annabel silently put knives and forks on the table, with crackers and all the tinsel and paraphernalia that makes Christmas special. They sat down to eat. Ruth was a wonderful cook.

'Now, it's time to tell me.'

The whole story emerged as her sister sat there, listening to every word while sipping her wine and eating her food.

'So you went to see this daughter?' Ruth whispered in amazement as the flames leapt from the Christmas pudding. 'Do you know where he lives?'

'Well, almost. I don't know. It's odd.'

'You've been there, to his house?'

'Once, but it's all dark and hazy. Nothing's clear.'

'Does he know you're pregnant?'

'No,'

'You haven't told him?' Ruth stared, open-mouthed, at her sister – the clever one.

'Moments evolve.'

'What are you going to do?' she murmured.

'I've no idea,'

'What do you want to do?'

'I've no idea.'

'What?' exclaimed Ruth.

'It's grotesque. She was there in darkness, all alone.'

'On Christmas Eve?'

'Yes, there were no lights until he turned one on, and then I saw her white, emaciated body. For a moment, a fleeting moment, I thought she was dead.'

'Did she speak?'

'No, she didn't. She ignored me altogether. She mumbled a few words to him, which I didn't hear.'

'Go on.'

'The atmosphere was dark. The air felt as if it contained some hidden being. I left.'

'What do you mean, hidden being?' Ruth whispered, utterly fascinated. 'Don't you believe me?'

'What do you mean?' she replied, feeling more and more intrigued.'

'A presence, an atmosphere even. Somehow, it's everywhere.'

'What's everywhere?'

Annabel's thoughts took on flights of their own. She picked up mince pies that lay on their side in the middle of the plate. She gazed at the icing sugar sprinkled on top and thought about the strangeness of it. She wondered if it had all been a dream. Had last night happened?

The mobile rang. It was Sam. She didn't pick up. There was a strange fascination. It was impossible to forget the woman and walk away. She had to know more of this man and his daughter. Was she mad? Did Sam keep her in prison there? Was there someone who checked on her, cared for her? Was it his way of protecting her? Perhaps she'd always been this way. Maybe her mother started to drink because of the pressure of looking after her. Sam had just left them alone and went on with his life. Yes, that must be it.

Why did he take me there last night? Didn't he realize it would upset me? Did he want to disturb everything? Why was I so stupid as to go to bed with this man in the first place? Geoffrey was safe. *Why did I rock the boat?* Did she really not know the answer? Could it be that this clever woman really didn't know?

There were one or two more presents to unwrap. She silently passed one to Ruth, but it was no good – her mind was elsewhere. It stayed with this woman. It would not be consoled or distracted.

'What about Handford?' asked Ruth at last.

At that moment, Annabel's mobile phone beeped. She had a message. She read it: 'Gone to see my daughter.'

'Where does his daughter live?'

'I don't know. I told you I don't know.'

Ruth picked up the dishes and loaded them into the dishwasher.

Thoughts sped across her mind at an alarming rate.

What do I want? wondered Annabel. *Never mind what I've done. Now I have to deal with the consequences.*

This time she'd overstepped the mark. She'd gone too far – she knew that. This grotesque situation threatened to overwhelm her, to destroy the fabric of her life. She craved the security that work provided; it kept her safe. It gave her a harbour. It had been her anchor through all the changing seas of life. She needed it as if it were a drug.

CHAPTER NINETEEN

Sam left his house and walked quickly. It was bitterly cold. The sun shone on the snow sculptures that lay all around. He placed his mind squarely on the entertainment nature had provided for him – the way the snow lay across the paths where others had walked since the night before. It was as though the hard ground beneath his feet, the frozen air in his nostrils, and the numbness of his face were there to remind him of what had gone before. It cut him as surely as the wind now cut his skin.

He thought of Annabel. He thought of her terror, of what had gone before, of what she had seen in that house, and of the arid sense of abandonment that pervaded the air. He supposed he had got used to it – he accepted it in the way people do. He'd adapted to it. It surrounded his waking and his sleeping. He acknowledged that Judith had become less angry since seeing John Antony. Now she'd retreated into herself. He wondered, as he walked, if that was, in fact, progress or regression. It was impossible to know, he concluded, impossible to know anything at all. Suddenly, inexplicably his mood changed. The cold air brought crisp, sharp hope.

He walked out of Kensington Gardens, crossed Bayswater Road, and slipped into the Greek Orthodox Church at the bottom of Moscow Road. The service was over, but the pungent smell of incense hung in the air. As he sat down, the sun shone through the windows onto the golden image of the icons. The strange darkness that had fallen across his life all those months before made him wonder if life would ever be whole again. He remembered clearly the certainty that is despair and how close he had come to danger in those dark months. The icons had been with him all the way, with their beauty and their mysterious yet compelling religiosity.

He left after half an hour or so and continued on to his daughter's flat, observing that the cold had gotten colder and the sky darker. Gently, snow fell around him as he walked. He knocked on the door. At first, he thought there was no one there, so he opened the door with his own key.

Chaos reigned within. The kitchen door stood ajar. He looked in to find the table littered with open jam jars and lumps of crusty bread. But most of all, there was an absence. Crockery lay piled up on the sink, on the worktops, everywhere. The bedroom door was wide open. The first thing he saw were folds of dark blue velvet covering her. Somehow the folds gave away her mortality. The garment he'd given her for Christmas covered her body. He sat down beside her and placed his arms around her. She was now so thin, so emaciated, that he could feel every bone. He placed his head in the velvet, absorbed the perfume that was around her, and cried. Hope evaporated once more.

****

Judith didn't speak. She lay there, surrounded by her father. She had never, ever felt so lonely, so desolate, or so weak. She got up and poured a drink for two, knocking the bottle against the glass and spilling the liquid on to the dark carpet.

What more is it that is hurting me? thought Judith.

The decision: It's over. I can't go on. There was, she realized, no way back. She could have a thousand conversations with John Antony, but they would make no difference whatsoever.

When one person kills another, they kill themselves too. She went about like someone sunk under lightness. A crazy laughter was emanating from her lips, spreading across her face.

'I'm not like the beast returning from market,' he said, 'because I always carry the same load.'

His sense of shame confused her.

'Didn't she ever disgust you? Didn't you ever wish her to be in the depths of hell?' Judith yelled.

'I was afraid she'd be gentle again. That's an awful fear, fear of the moment when she would turn her words into something between us that no one else could ever share. She would say, "You have to stay with me. Without you, I can't live." Then she'd turn and scream that I was the devil, that I made her old and dirty. I'd ask her if she meant it, and she'd say yes. She was drunk. I often walked away wishing that she'd die, and then she'd be quiet and not take my heart and soul again. The thing was, she was only mine when she was truly drunk. I didn't believe that her life was as it was, and the fact that I didn't proves that there is something wrong with me. I was like a shadow in her dream that could never reach her in time. The cry of the sleeper has no echo. She was like a new shadow walking perilously close to the outer curtain, and I was going mad because I was awake, seeing it, unable to reach it.'

'I didn't know. I didn't know that it was to be me who was to do the terrible thing. I saw her before my eyes, corrupt and withering. I went mad. I've been mad ever since, and there's nothing to do – nothing!' Judith screamed.

'Stop it! Stop it!' he cried. 'You're a good woman. She was outside the human type, a wild thing caught up in human skin, monstrously alone. After Harry's death, she was monstrously alone. She was a paralysed creature, lined with velvet. This was where you learnt wisdom, where you learnt to give death.'

Her father would soon leave. Until that moment came, she would be kind, but her mind was made up. That priceless galaxy of misinformation called the mind, harnessed itself to the conglomerate known as the soul, and led her on to the path of destruction.

What, she thought to herself, *are the things I must do? What are the things I want to see?* Her mind drifted around possibilities. The round pond – she wanted to go there and see the ducks, to cross Hyde Park in the cold winter air. There would be seconds of terror, and seconds later it would be gone. What would she wear? Black, of course, but the velvet coat and dress were not warm enough. The possibility of many under layers occupied her mind for minutes, and then there would be the colour of the layers and also the thickness. How thick would they have to be? How thick and how long? What time of day – morning, afternoon, or evening? It had to be in daylight; otherwise, she wouldn't be able to see the ducks on the pond.

Death, she thought, what risk is there with death? What risk is there to take? What part of me will die first – my hands or my feet? I thought Claude and I were so much in love that these moments couldn't happen. But happen they do, without celebration. Love does not protect you from actions. It cannot protect you from yourself. Love is raw.

'She knew she was driving me insane with misery and fright,' said Sam. 'I have been loved by something strange. It forgot me; it forgot you.'

'I've done and been everything I didn't want to do and be, so I stand here, beaten up, mauled, and weeping – knowing I am not what I thought I was,' she murmured.

'Are any of us what we think we are?'

****

The following day, her father was gone, as she had known he would be. There were many moments of softness and gentle crying. Those times arrived for Judith at that time and in that place. It was not as difficult as it had been before the decision was made. There was no more wondering, *What happens now? Where do I go from here? How do I move on?* There was no moving on.

She showered and got dressed. Clean black underwear lay on her bed, ready, along with a cosy grey sweater. She wanted to be cosy and cosseted, and this was her cosiest garment. She put her long black velvet coat on, locked the flat, and left. It was so cold. She felt the frozen air enter her being. She walked very slowly; she didn't want to miss anything on this white day.

The ducks were there, as they always were. She watched them. People came and went.

It was not as long or as difficult as she had, at first, imagined it to be; there was a peace. She arrived at the underground at Marble Arch. The display panel showed that the next train would arrive in four minutes. She waited. The panel then said there had been a delay and the train would not be along for fifteen minutes. Judith noticed orange silk gowns lined with Tibetan red. The monks stood close to her as she moved to the edge of the platform. One of the men approached.

'Take care. You're a little close,' he said with smiling eyes.

The train approached. Judith took one step towards the platform edge when she heard the train. The man with the smiling eyes put out his arm. 'No!' he said. It was a command, rather than a request, which she felt compelled to obey. She drew back. The monk stayed with her as the people boarded the train and it left the station.

'Do not commit such violence against yourself.'

How, she wondered, *can you be so soft and yet so strong?* 'It's my life. It belongs to me,' she murmured.

'No,' he replied. 'You are a part of the universe. Your actions reverberate through all creation.' He led her away from the platform. 'What has made you feel this way?'

'I killed someone,'

'You think you can make it right by killing yourself?'

'What else is there?'

'Compassion – compassion for yourself and for the person you killed.' Judith thought for moments about what the monk had said – that she was in some way linked to the universe and all that it contained. She was a part of it; that was how she'd felt when she loved Claude and, even before that, when she'd painted. The monk stood close to her, holding on to her. Nothing she could say could make him let go of her.

The thing had become impossible. She'd been stopped in her tracks. There was nothing for her and nowhere for her to go. Slowly and silently, the monk led her out of the station and into the cold air. She felt thwarted, angry even, but there was something indefinable about this monk who compelled compliance.

They walked silently across Hyde Park into Bayswater Road. He kept hold of her arm all the way home. He invited himself in, locked the flat, and sat silently on the floor. Judith just stared at him. His presence soothed her. She made tea and gave him a cup. He bowed to her as he took it from her hand.

'Why did you bow to me?' she asked.

'You have given me a gift,' he replied.

'Are you staying?' she asked, feeling powerless in his presence.

'As long as I am needed, I will stay,' he replied.

'How long will that be?'

'Until someone arrives who can care for you. I will know when that person arrives.'

'If I phone someone, how about that, and they come to see me?' 'It depends,' he replied.

'What does it depend on?'

'If they are the right person: I will not know that until they arrive.'

'I'll phone John Antony, shall I?'

'If you think he's the one to care for you.'

Judith phoned him, but there was no answer.

'We wait,' said the monk. 'Someone will come.'

'How do you know?' she asked, sitting close to him.

'They will arrive.'

Chapter twenty

Nausea washed over Annabel. She hardly knew this woman but somehow she felt involved in her life – grotesque and hideous though it was. Annabel was determined not to be alone, yet she didn't want companionship. She turned off her mobile phone and wandered aimlessly from one place to another through London streets. Some were noisy; some were busy. There was the general buzz of humanity at sales time.

Annabel thought a little about her parents in the Hebrides. Life hadn't made sense. Nothing made sense. Life itself became a farce until she got to university on the mainland. Maths, on the other hand, always made sense. It had a logic that no other aspect of her life possessed, and so she had clung to it. It had become her passion. Nothing at that time would have persuaded her to abandon her studies at the university. Maths contained her. It held its own beauty.

Judith made no sense, and this situation, made no sense. It was bleak, dark, and pointless.

I'll go and see her. That's what I'll do. What do I have to lose? The worst that can happen is that she will refuse to let me in.

****

Annabel knocked at the front door. Judith emerged, covered in a thick woollen shawl.

'Go away.'

'Please let me in. I just want to talk,' Annabel pleaded.

'What about?'

'You. I just want to talk about you.'

'I don't want——'

'Let the person in,' commanded the monk.

'Look, it's bitterly cold out here. Couldn't we just have a cup of coffee?' Annabel pleaded.

Judith relented and opened the door, and Annabel went in. Judith looked in amazement at the monk. His eyes met hers. He stared at her for seconds, and then he stood up and left. The lounge, Annabel noticed, had a large fire, soft sofas, and bits of this and that strewn around in disarray – books, pencils, drawings, and paper.

'You were here with my father the other night, weren't you? Christmas Eve,' Judith said after bidding farewell to the monk.

'Yes, that's right.'

She went into the kitchen to make the coffee. Annabel looked at the pictures. The walls were covered with paintings of olive trees. As she sat down, Judith returned with a large cafetière, a jug of milk, and two mugs. She poured out the hot steaming liquid and passed a mug to Annabel. It smelt thick and heavy.

'This coffee is exquisite,' Annabel murmured as she looked at Judith. She thought there was much about her that was exquisite – the long, slender hands; the bone structure of her face; and last, but by no means least, the eyes – they were like vast orbs in the centre of her face, a deep violet colour, almost black. She'd not seen any of this the night before. Now Sam's daughter looked very different.

'Yes, it's good coffee. I buy it from a stall in Portobello Road.'

'When I saw you the other night, I thought you were ill. I wondered if that was why you were alone,' Annabel murmured.

'No, that's not true. When you saw me the other night, you thought I was grotesque. That's why you left. I frightened you…didn't I?'

'I felt I was intruding, that I wasn't meant to be here.'

'Well, you're here now. What's changed?' she demanded.

'I don't know exactly. Have you never had that experience – you do something and you don't know why?'

'Maybe, I'm not sure,' Judith murmured, remembering vividly that day…that awful day.

'It may have been curiosity that drew me back. God knows.'

'How do you know my father?' she asked, drawing the woollen shawl more tightly around herself.

'We met one day,' Annabel whispered in a voice that was hardly audible.

'Where?'

'In a cafe.'

'What were you doing there?'

'I was drinking coffee and crying.'

'Why were you crying?' Judith asked, placing two large logs in the wood stove, which crackled and sent sparks into the air.

'Oh, you know. The usual things,' Annabel replied.

'Go on. Tell me.'

'Man problems, exhaustion I kept crying, and your father came and sat beside me. We started to talk. He said his wife had died recently. He was sad too and said he wished he could cry as I did.'

'Oh,' Judith whispered, feeling surprisingly touched.

'His wife…she must have been your mother. I'm so sorry.'

'Don't be. I'm not!' Judith snapped.

'No, mothers are complicated creatures, aren't they? Mine is very odd, lives in the Hebrides. If she died, I don't think I'd notice.'

Judith felt herself irresistibly drawn to this woman's disarming honesty. 'Really? Don't you like her?' she asked.

'No, if I really think about it, I don't believe I do,' Annabel replied slowly, weighing every word.

'Why not?'

'Well, there isn't much to like or dislike for that matter.'

'I see,' replied Judith, smiling to herself. This woman was mysteriously amusing.

'Didn't you like yours either?'

'No. Would you like some bread and jam?' she enquired, changing the subject.

Annabel's mind went back to the day in bed with Sam when he made her toast and jam. She couldn't stop smiling. 'Yes, please, that'd be wonderful.'

Judith went to the kitchen, found a loaf of white crusty bread, and placed it on a tray with butter, knives, and three pots of jam.

'Well, that's something we both have in common,' said Annabel. 'Neither of us likes our mothers.'

'No,' Judith sliced the bread as she spoke.

'What about your father?'

'I love him.'

The two women fell silent as they buttered their bread and chose their jam. Annabel chose plum.

She's a bit like a plum, thought Judith. That's exactly the right choice for her. A bit of fruit fell off Annabel's bread and landed on the floor.

'Oh, sorry,' she muttered, trying to remove it with a tissue and making it worse. 'Oh dear.'

'Never mind.'

'Will you help me?' Annabel said, at last. 'I'm in such a bloody mess and I don't know what to do.'

'Help you? Me, help you?' Judith replied in amazement. 'Not me, not me – I can't help anyone.'

'I'm in such a mess. It's all my own fault. I don't think anyone else can help me.'

'Well, I don't think——'

'Please help me,'

'I'll listen.: that's all I can promise.'

'Will you try not to judge me?' Annabel asked.

'I'm in no position to judge anyone,' Judith said slowly, deliberately, and darkly.

Annabel began her story with Claude and how their relationship had deteriorated once his grief dissipated. She added, almost incidentally, that he'd gone to France to teach van Gogh and met someone else. Judith could scarcely believe what she was hearing. Her eyes opened, glazing over. She hardly heard Annabel saying that she'd found a job and was offered promotion if she agreed to move to Handford.

'I studied statistical analysis and maths at university, you see. I specialized in health economics for my MA.'

'Go on. Do go on,' Judith pleaded, utterly mesmerized by the story this woman was relating. She threw more logs into the wood-burning stove, piled a couple of cushions behind her back, and made herself as comfortable as she could. Oh my God! she thought. It was extraordinary how the story, and Annabel herself, animated and excited her.

'You see, it's not clear,' Annabel went on. 'I met Geoffrey, who had this lovely house in the country, and it was all going well, at least so I thought, but it seemed wrong. Something wasn't right,' she said slowly.

'What do you mean?' Judith asked.

'He kept on and on. I felt him invading my privacy, my personal space, but I enjoyed being at his house. It was so beautiful. Then I couldn't work out whether it was him or his house I loved. It was the perfect space to escape from the pressures of work. Do you see? You do see that, don't you?'

'I think so.'

'Well, then I came back to London for ten days' leave in October and stayed with my sister. That was when I met your father.'

'In the cafe?' she enquired.

'Yes, that's right,'

'You were crying?'

'Yes. I'd seen him a few days before when I was with my sister. We often went there. The coffee is so good, and so are the cakes.'

'Go on,' Judith commanded.

'Maybe I shouldn't tell you the rest.'

'How can I help if you don't?'

'Well it might be the…end of us, the end of everything,'

'I doubt that. You think something is the end of everything, and then you realize that it's not. It could, in fact, be the very opposite,' Judith replied slowly, amazed at her response.

'I don't know how it happened. Well, that's not true. It happened because we both wanted it to happen. He wanted comfort and I wanted…him,' Annabel murmured.

'You went to bed with him? With my father?' exclaimed Judith.

'Yes, yes, I did. I'm sorry. No, I'm not sorry at all, not really. I want you to forgive me. I don't know why: I just do that's why I had to come.'

There was silence for a few moments.

'I'm stunned.'

'I know. I know what I did was stupid. I didn't think about the consequences.'

'What do you mean, the consequences?'

'I don't know. I've told you so much, maybe we should leave it.' 'Nothing you've done could be—'

'I don't understand myself, not at all. Your father is just…'

'No, you've got me completely wrong,' Judith replied, looking at the floor.

'I don't know where to turn. My sister is shocked by my stupidity and my recklessness : so am I.'

'We all do terrible things. Just tell me what you mean by consequences.' 'I'm pregnant. Your father is——'

'What? Oh my God! Does he know?' she exclaimed.

'No, no he doesn't. You see, I have to decide very quickly whether to keep the baby or resume my previous life and just go back to my job in Handford. Perhaps I should get rid of it, say nothing to your father, and go back to my job,'

'I'm begging you. Don't get rid of the child. Please…please.'

'Why, don't you think I should?'

'I want to help you, perhaps you're right – perhaps I can help you.

My father has suffered a good deal in the last few months since… And I think this news could be just what he needs, perhaps it was meant to be. I believe in fate. Do you?'

Annabel didn't answer. She stared into the fire.

'We only went to bed once. It was impetuous,' she whispered. Tears ran down her face.

Judith felt warmth and compassion for this stranger. She had not known this feeling for months, not since that day… Heat rose in her belly and spread itself around her body every cell in her responded to Annabel.

'Don't get rid of it and go back to Handford. I didn't mean to make the decision for you, but I have. I've made the decision for you.' Judith put her arm around Annabel. They watched the fire in silence for a long, long time.

'I'm glad for my father perhaps he could be happy at last. You'll give him life, a second chance. You were sent into our lives to restore.

It's not just buildings and paintings that need restoring – people do, too.'

'What about you? Tell me about you. Do you need restoring?'

'You don't want to know about me; you really don't. I'm beyond restoration. I can never, ever be restored.'

'I do. I want to know about you,' Annabel murmured. 'Why were you all alone on Christmas Eve?'

'What I've done is the very opposite of what you've done.'

Annabel gazed at Judith's face lit up by the glow from the fire and thought how beautiful it must have been once, before the shadows took up residence underneath her eyes, the grey pallor tainted her skin, the haunted look usurped her. This woman was old before her time. Why, Annabel wondered, did she look so deadened? It was as if someone had smeared white putty mixed with ivory powder all over her face, as if a thick mask sat on her skin. Her eyes resembled the darkest ebony; they had the look of the hunted, the depraved, and the ravaged.

Suddenly Judith said she wanted some more bread, got up, and walked towards the kitchen.

Then she retraced her steps., There was something about this woman that had completely disarmed her. The two women looked at one another.

'What is the worst thing that one human being can do to another?' she asked.

'Kill them, I suppose.'

'That's what I did.'

Annabel didn't answer. She looked, and then she looked again. 'Some people deserve to be murdered. Mr Reynolds deserved to be murdered,' she murmured, staring into the flames of the fire.

'You don't really believe that, do you?' Judith murmured.

'Of course I do. Doesn't every intelligent person believe that? Think about it just for a moment. You must have been…hurt beyond endurance by this person. Perhaps people who cause that much agony deserve to be killed, and then the victims of their behaviour are set free to live, to love…whatever. It's a way of gaining freedom,'

'Some people think that life is sacred. Don't you?'

'There are no absolutes. Absolutes are for the stupid,' she replied.

'Tell me, Annabel, how did you come to be so wise?'

'Me, wise? No, I don't think so. It's just that I'm such a mess. I make so many mistakes with relationships. I'm always doing the wrong thing, but I don't mean to.'

'You're the best thing that's happened to me in a long, long time – maybe ever. It's like you're a housewife come to set straight disorder in a messed-up house,' she whispered. 'Don't you want to know who I killed and why?'

'Not really. I know whoever it was deserved it, or you wouldn't have done it. That much I do know.'

'Don't you think I should be punished? Sent to prison or something?' 'From what I saw the other night, you've been punished enough. Let go of it. Go on with your life,' Annabel replied.

Judith looked at her and thought about the monk who'd saved her and about this woman who'd mysteriously arrived as if from nowhere, with some unknown power. *It's like some benevolent force has come towards me*, she thought.

'I have to go back to Handford.'

'I'm begging you not to go. Please don't leave us.' 'It's only until May.'

'The darkness will return. I know it will.'

'No, it won't be the same. We can talk every day.' 'Will you stay here with me?'

'I'll stay with you tonight,' Annabel replied.

Judith gave her some sheets and made up the bed. Annabel phoned her sister and said she was staying with a friend, switching off the mobile before Ruth could ask any more questions. She lay in the flat that night hidden from the world – no one knew where she was. In a very real sense, she didn't know where she was. Yet there was a sense of rightness about it, as if – at last – she knew where she was supposed to be. This instinctive visit to Judith had led her to a knowledge that was primal, about belonging. Words, as they so often did, crept unbidden into her mind. The wolf that never howls never finds its pack, she thought. She went to sleep that night knowing, for the first time in her life, that she was exactly where she was meant to be.

Judith phoned her father, 'Annabel's here. It's wonderful,' she said.

CHAPTER TWENTY ONE

The next morning, Annabel forced herself to return to work. She drove from London with a heavy heart. The journey seemed long and arduous. The weather conditions made for slow progress, but at least it gave her time to think, time to just be. She put Adele on her stereo and then James Arthur, whose grating, caustic voice she adored. His newly released single 'Impossible' summed up the entire scenario – it was, indeed, impossible. She drove along the M4, and her thoughts turned to murder and, inevitably, to murderers, the books she'd read, the real-life murderers she'd heard of.

She'd met a real murderer; it slowly closed around her mind, this concept, this truth, this reality. She approached Swindon and knew that she had to return to London and tell Sam about the pregnancy. Sometimes, things happen in life that are so huge that they smother everything that has ever gone before. They obliterate any earlier existence. They become your existence. This, she knew, was such a time. It felt as if she had been chosen by some invisible force to be with these two people who were, in many ways, wretched.

****

Sam walked towards his daughter's flat. Judith told him everything that Annabel had said – that some people deserved to be murdered and that she thought murderers were, in certain circumstances, liberators. Sam turned this over and over in his head. Had his wife deserved to be murdered? He thought it an extreme point of view, but he couldn't utterly dismiss it. After all, Virginia had been given every opportunity to recover, but she'd made little, if any, effort. He realized quite suddenly that, in a sense, Annabel had turned Judith into a heroine. She had exonerated her and, by so doing, had set her free. He mused on the words of David Hume, 'Beauty lies nowhere but in the eyes of the beholder.'

Maybe, he thought, the same is true of evil. That, too, lies nowhere but in the eye of the beholder.

When Judith told him about the pregnancy, Sam's mind went into overdrive. He was deeply shocked and, at the same, time confused and somewhat disorientated. Everything in him stopped. It was Judith's eyes, the way she looked at him that made him reel. It was as if the news of this birth had infused Judith with new life.

****

It was at this time that he decided to sell. He wanted to make the decision alone, without advice from anyone. It was the family home. It was the place where his wife had been murdered. He did not want his child to live in it. It would take time, but that was fine. He didn't have to stay in his house. He would rent somewhere and put the house on the market.

Once the decision had been made, he was desperate to get rid of it. Every day he phoned the estate agent to see if there was any interest. He accepted the first offer, though it was below the asking price; he didn't care. The idea that he owned it suddenly sickened him. He wanted to be rid of it before his child was born.

'There is nothing to be said, nothing to be done. I want it all to be gone,' he said one morning to John Antony.

'It's as if you're frightened of it, of the past and your part in it.'

'I am. I've made the most hideous mistakes a man can make. I run away when I can't handle things.'

'What can't you handle now?'

'Self-loathing is never far away from me. I just want to be in a place where I can walk and write. I don't want to have to make decisions about property deals, decoration, or any of the normal things. I just want to think and write – a kind of penance, contemplation. I have to absorb and to integrate what has happened. Why have I been given this second chance?'

'Yet there is the light, more than you have realized.'

'It is invisible to me,' Sam murmured.

'Where will you live, do you imagine?'

'Somewhere old., It will have to be very old indeed. There will be green space around so that I can walk and experience nature – a contrast to the darkness of my past existence.'

'Have you ever considered the good you could do...if you wanted to?' John asked.

'How do you mean? How could I do good?'

'Think about it for a moment, you're a rich man. Rich men can always do good if they want to.'

'Go on.'

'Well, it's not impossible to envisage. It depends on whether you want to keep your business or not.'

'Yes, of course it does. Everything depends on that. I've lost heart and lost interest in everything. I've been thinking of selling all my property as a matter of fact and just keeping a home for Judith and me.'

'Have you ever thought of opening a unit?' John said slowly, giving every syllable as much weight as possible.

'A unit? What, for alcoholics and their families? Is that what you mean?' 'Well, it would be worth consideration...wouldn't it?'

'It would be a form of absolution,' Sam whispered, almost to himself. He was to acknowledge his part in it all – running away when he should have stayed. He'd found ways to escape from the suffering of both his wife and his daughter. He had failed them both in the most hideous way. Yet, the universe had inexplicably forgiven him. Annabel had appeared as if from nowhere. The sun lit up the garden. No one in the world could understand what had happened to them; only the two of them could understand, and that, in itself, was proof that they were right.

****

April appeared in wondrous apparel and with uncharacteristic warmth. Plants and hedgerows burst into flower. For the first week, there was no rain. Sam got out maps and browsed the computer for places that would meet his exact requirements. He also had long conversations with John Antony, who had become both his friend and his confidant, through which they tried to work towards something close to comprehension.

'If I sell all my property, I'll be able to open a unit for addicts, a place where families can go for succour and for strength. I've decided that's what I'm going to do,' Sam said one day as they were sitting in the bright April sunshine, gazing at the daffodils all around them.

He'd had this idea in his mind for several days. It had taken time to germinate, to grow roots within his being, but it was there. It was becoming clearer in his mind's eye and was gaining a reality, which would deepen if shared.

He would look for somewhere after his business had been sold. Possibly, it would be an old property – an old school or a manor house ripe for renovation. Alternatively, a new unit, purpose-built, might prove the best option of all. He knew a lot of architects and surveyors who would provide all the expertise he required. His nephew Thomas Steel was a civil engineer, and had fulfilled contracts for the NHS.

This was a way of making amends, a way for him to atone and to help other people who found themselves facing the same dilemma that he had faced. He thought of his daughter; he was slowly gaining a foothold into her psyche. He was tiptoeing along the threshold of her mind – insight, and even compassion, were taking root.

This was helped by the arrival of Annabel in his life. He looked on her as a miracle or a gift or, indeed, both. He knew that, despite everything he'd done or failed to do, fortune had smiled on him. He was to be a father once more. He was to be a husband once more. And all because, one day, a pretty lady had cried in a cafe, and he'd felt pity for her, and then he'd felt desire. She smelt of almonds, vanilla, and roses her skin was soft and powdery, like silk. He thought of touching it. He thought of the cream velvet-crushed gardenia that was Annabel.

'Are you any closer to understanding why she did it?' Sam asked as he sat in the garden with John Antony.

'The idea formed in Judith's mind a long time ago. It was conceived when she was a child,' John replied.

'What idea?'

'The idea, the ambition if you like, to kill her mother. She was given the chance to commit the perfect murder, and she took it.'

'Did she say that?'

'Yes, on many occasions.'

Sam fell silent for a while, staring at the green grass beneath his feet, pondering, absorbing John's words. They shocked and saddened him. What, he wondered, would it be like to want to kill your own mother?

'Are you saying that she wanted to murder her when she was a little girl?'

'She was fascinated by graveyards. That's why she painted them all the time. I remember the first time I saw one she'd painted. It had one hundred and one different shades of green and one hundred and one gravestones.'

'Yes, the mystery of green.'

'Freud spoke about the death wish, you know. I believe in Judith it was particularly strong. With most people, it's buried deep in the unconscious mind.'

'I see. Why do you think that was?'

'I believe, though I may be wrong, that when she was very, very young – possibly even when she was a baby – she was terrified of her mother,'

'Harry died. Virginia never got over it. I tried to console her, but it was no good.'

'They call it the' mourning mother syndrome'. The mother's emotional energy is entirely taken up with the grieving process. She is unable to bond with the baby.'

Sam got up and left as his mind slipped back to thoughts of Harry, that dear little chap every sense had intensified since he'd made love to Annabel, every emotion heightened. He gazed at the clumps of daffodils all around him. The yellow burnt into his being as if he were internalizing the rays of the sun. Eventually, he returned to the house and picked up his Blackberry. He saw the estate agent had called three times and left an email telling him the house had been sold. He breathed a sigh of relief. 'Thank God,' he emailed back. The house where Virginia had died – the place where she had been killed – was going out of his life. Tremors of joy shot across his entire being. He needed to be alone, to think and to be.

He went upstairs to his computer and looked for old properties near open spaces. It seemed there was just one, but it was the other side of London, on the edge of Hampstead Heath. He got into his car, turned on his satnav, entered the postcode, and drove there. At last he arrived at a rambling house that was covered with ivy. He leant on the garden gate and looked in. A large oak tree stood in the centre, and a couple of elderly benches sat beneath its branches. There was a very large front door with a bell that you pulled. He looked up at the front of the house. Beneath the ivy were windows of various shapes and sizes. Some were small, some were big, some medium-sized; some had lead between the panes of glass, and some did not. It was what one would describe as higgledy-piggledy.

Something here fascinated him, drew him like a magnet. He phoned the estate agent at once and was told that it was empty and that he could view immediately. A young man arrived with the keys, and in they went. The first thing that was apparent was that the ivy had crept through the windowpanes. It was everywhere. The kitchen had wooden floors, which were covered with dust that had clearly been there for a long time. There was a huge old cupboard with woodcarvings and an Aga, the old-fashioned cream type, and some wooden worktops accommodating trailing ivy that had crept in through the large kitchen window. The window looked out directly onto the oak tree, which was, in fact, so extensive that it was impossible to see either beyond it or to the side of it. In an extraordinary way, it was part of the house. Oak House – Sam could see that it could never have any other name.

The hall had only a small window with leaded glass, which was inadequate for lighting. The one room, which had clearly been the main living area, had a vast window that looked out on to Hampstead Heath. It was a bright sunny day, and the light flooded the room. Sam glanced at the walls around him and saw old bookcases that had been left to their own devices. He thought how strange and lonely they looked without books – sad and abandoned.

There was another smaller room downstairs. Here, too, ivy trailed through the window, and the room contained no furniture at all. He and the estate agent proceeded up to a small landing, where there was a heavily beamed room with an old desk and, again, masses of bookcases covered with a mixture of dust and ivy. The window, once again, looked out on to the oak tree on the front lawn. This place comforted him.

Mr Villars, the agent, led the way up the stairs to an old bathroom, which had a small leaded window and a four-legged bath. An assortment of tiles on the wall depicted English country life at the turn of the nineteenth century. Sam thought they were almost certainly Victorian. They proceeded to a succession of bedrooms of various shapes and sizes. Three were large, one looked out onto the oak tree and one onto the expanse of Hampstead Heath. Mr Villars said the house had been on the market for four months. The last owner had lived there for all of his ninety years and had raised his family there – two children, in fact. One had emigrated to Canada, and the other to New Zealand.

The surveyor's report came back as 'satisfactory', as could be expected under the circumstances, and the sale went ahead with no further delays. It appeared that the children were keen to sell and were delighted at receiving the asking price.

****

Annabel, meanwhile, was struggling with both her work and her pregnancy. She felt life lying heavily across her back at this time, and yet she didn't know why.

I used to enjoy my work. It used to interest me, she mused. It doesn't any more.

She missed Sam. She and Judith spoke every day, and it was the moment she enjoyed most. Sometimes, though rarely, she thought of Claude, who had gone to France and rented a flat in Paris, in the rue de l'Odéon. He sent her the odd postcard. He said Paris was ideal for painting and for his recovery. He described the walks he had in the bohemian district, the cafes, the galleries, and the antiquated bookshops.

May arrived at last, and Annabel's contract in Handford ended. She gleefully packed her belongings into her car and set off for London. When she arrived, Sam was at Oak House, waiting for her. It was dishevelled – as, indeed, was she – but she loved it. He carried her into the bedroom, and everything he'd held in for all those years burst out. She cried and bellowed as he held her and steadied her with his strong hands. They made love, writhing carefully so as not to hurt the little fingerling inside her. Sam, with his sweet smell, his large hands and his unequivocal body wanting her, wanting her... How she had missed that protruding desire. She answered him with torrents of passion she didn't know a pregnant woman was capable of.

Dawn broke. They walked arm in arm down the path from the house and saw the massive oak tree before them. The elderly benches welcomed them as they watched the sunrise.

'I've decided to sell everything, all my property. This place will be properly restored, but the main thing I have to tell you is that I intend to invest much of the money in a purpose-built unit for recovering alcoholics. There'll also be a unit for the families of alcoholics, a place they can come to where they'll be supported and where they can feel safe and at peace. I've no idea at the moment where it will be.'

Annabel fell into deep thought about this decision. What else could he do? It was so very much the correct conclusion. And all that had to be understood would be understood eventually – over time.

About The Author

Mollie is a health advisor. She has experienced the world of addiction from a personal and professional perspective. She is a psychiatric nurse advisor and has worked both at The Maudsley Hospital, where she trained, and at The Priory Hospital, where she ran addiction groups both for alcoholics and their families.

Mollie's parents both committed suicide when she was a child.

It is both her work and her past that has motivated her to write this novel.

Acknowledgment

Lyn Webster Wilde: B.A. Cambridge University/Literary advisor and mentor. Elinor Martell : Managing director at RENNAISANCE ART RETREATS. Freud Sigmund: The interpretation of Dreams.

Carl Jung: On the Nature of the Psyche.

John Clare and Ali Zarbafi: Social dreaming in the 21st century. Jonathon Lear: Love and it's place in nature.

Derek Fell:Van Gogh's Women

RA. The real Van Gogh;The artist and his letters.

Charlotte Dyne Steel Artist /Tutor.